Cognitive-Behavioral Therapy (CBT) For Beginners

Break free from negative patterns and transform your life.

Author: Joseph Rabie

D1714811

Updated January 2024
Legal deposit January 2024

Table of contents

Introduction

Are you ready to discover a powerful approach that will enable you to take control of your mind, change undesirable behaviors, and create a fulfilling and satisfying life? Welcome to the world of cognitive-behavioral therapy. This book is specially designed for beginners who wish to explore the foundations of cognitive-behavioral therapy (CBT) and derive tangible benefits from it. Whether you're dealing with anxiety, depression, eating disorders, phobias, or any other emotional challenge, this comprehensive guide will help you understand and apply the essential principles of CBT to transform your life.

Cognitive-behavioral therapy is a widely recognized and effective therapeutic approach based on the idea that our thoughts, emotions, and behaviors are closely interconnected. By understanding these connections and using specific techniques, you can identify and modify negative thought patterns and destructive behaviors that limit you.

In this book, we will guide you through the basics of CBT, explaining the fundamental principles that underlie this approach in clear and accessible terms. You will learn to recognize the automatic thought patterns that fuel your negative emotions and discover how to restructure them in a constructive way. You will also explore behavioral techniques such as exposure and response prevention, which will help you overcome fears and limiting behaviors.

The strength of this book lies in its pragmatism. We will provide you with practical tools, exercises, and real-life examples to help you implement CBT concepts in your daily life. You will learn to develop clear therapeutic goals and plan your own treatment program, adapting techniques to the specific challenges you face.

Furthermore, we will also address specific applications of CBT for common issues such as anxiety, depression, eating disorders, and many others. You will discover how this approach can be adapted to different contexts and situations, offering a holistic perspective on your mental well-being.

Whether you are a complete novice in therapy or have some prior experience, this book will provide you with in-depth knowledge and practical guidance to start your journey towards a more balanced and fulfilling life. By applying the principles of CBT, you will be able to overcome your obstacles, change limiting thought patterns, and create new possibilities for yourself.
It's time to take control of your mental and emotional well-being. Get ready to explore the wonders of cognitive-behavioral therapy and unleash your full potential. This book is your essential guide to kickstart your journey towards lasting personal transformation. Prepare to discover the power of cognitive-behavioral therapy and take control of your life starting today.

Understanding Cognitive-Behavioral Therapy

▌ 1.1 What is Cognitive-Behavioral Therapy?

Cognitive-Behavioral Therapy (CBT) is a therapeutic approach based on the principle that our thoughts, emotions, and behaviors interact and influence our mental well-being. It aims to identify and modify negative thought patterns and maladaptive behaviors that contribute to psychological and emotional problems. CBT is built on the idea that our automatic thoughts, which are thoughts that spontaneously come to our mind, can significantly impact our mood and behavior. If we tend to have negative or irrational thoughts, it can lead to negative emotions and unhealthy behaviors. Therefore, CBT seeks to identify these automatic thoughts and replace them with more realistic and positive thoughts. Additionally, CBT emphasizes observable behavior. It acknowledges that our actions and behaviors can contribute to maintaining our psychological problems. Therefore, CBT uses behavioral techniques such as graduated exposure, response prevention, and social skills training to help individuals modify their problematic behaviors.

A bit of history:

Cognitive-Behavioral Therapy (CBT) was developed in the 1960s by several psychologists and psychiatrists. Aaron T. Beck, an American psychiatrist, is considered one of the key founders of CBT. He initially developed this therapeutic approach to treat depression, but its use later expanded to other psychological disorders.

The exact circumstances of its creation may vary according to sources, but in general, CBT was born out of a desire to find alternatives to the dominant psychoanalytic and psychodynamic approaches of the time. Early research highlighted the importance of thoughts and behaviors in the development and maintenance of psychological disorders, which led to the development of CBT.

Aaron T. Beck observed that depressed patients had negative and distorted thought patterns contributing to their emotional distress. He developed techniques to help patients identify and challenge these thought patterns, giving rise to cognitive therapy. Simultaneously, other psychologists worked on the behavioral aspect, using techniques such as classical and operant conditioning to address problematic behaviors. The combination of these approaches led to the creation of CBT, which integrates both cognitive and behavioral aspects.

Since its inception, CBT has been extensively studied and developed. It has become one of the most widely used and effective therapeutic approaches for a variety of psychological disorders.

1.2 The Fundamental Principles of Cognitive-Behavioral Therapy

CBT is based on several fundamental principles that guide its therapeutic approach:

1. Cognition Influences Emotion and Behavior:

Cognitive-Behavioral Therapy (CBT) is based on the principle that our thoughts, emotions, and behaviors are interconnected. Cognition, our thought process, directly influences our emotions and behaviors. CBT recognizes that negative thought patterns, cognitive distortions, and unrealistic beliefs can contribute to the development and maintenance of psychological problems such as depression, anxiety, phobias, and more. When we have negative or irrational thoughts, they can trigger negative emotions such as sadness, fear, anger, and so on. For example, if we have an irrational belief like *"I am a total failure,"* it can generate feelings of devaluation and discouragement. These emotions, in turn, influence our behaviors, such as avoiding challenging situations, procrastination, aggressiveness, and more.

CBT aims to identify and challenge these negative thought patterns in order to replace them with more realistic and positive thoughts. By altering our thoughts, we can positively influence our emotions and behaviors. For example, if we are able to question the irrational belief *"I am a total failure"* and replace it with a more realistic thought like *"I have experienced failures, but I have also succeeded in some situations,"* we can begin to experience increased self-esteem and enhanced motivation to overcome challenges.

Practical Sheet 1:
Step 1: Identification of Negative Thought Patterns

- Become aware of your recurring negative thoughts in specific situations.
- Identify cognitive distortions, such as overgeneralization, dichotomous thinking (all or nothing), selective filtering, etc.

Example: *"I am terrible in public. I will surely stutter, and everyone will judge me."*

Step 2: Evaluating the Evidence

- Ask yourself if there is concrete evidence to support your negative thoughts.
- Examine your past experiences, successes, and moments when your negative thoughts did not come true.

Example: *"Are there moments when I have successfully expressed myself in public without any issues?"*

Step 3: Replacing Negative Thought Patterns

- Generate alternative and more realistic thoughts to replace negative thought patterns.
- Use logical and objective arguments to counter cognitive distortions.

Example: *"I can prepare in advance, practice my speech, and remind myself that everyone makes mistakes. People will be more forgiving than I think."*

Step 4: Practice New Thoughts

- Regularly practice using your new realistic thoughts in situations that usually trigger negative thoughts.
- Take note of the differences you notice in your emotions and behaviors.

Example: Practice your speech while recalling your new realistic thoughts and observe how it affects your confidence and your ability to communicate effectively.

By following these steps of CBT, you can begin to change your negative thought patterns, thereby positively influencing your emotions and behaviors. It is important to practice regularly and exercise patience, as it may take time to anchor these new thought patterns in your daily life.

2. Present Moment Focus:

Cognitive Behavioral Therapy (CBT) is characterized by its focus on the present, which means it emphasizes current issues and present symptoms rather than exclusively dwelling on past events. This approach is based on several psychological principles.

1) **The Significance of the Here and Now:** CBT is based on the principle that psychological problems are often rooted in current thought patterns and behaviors. By focusing on the present, therapists can help individuals identify specific challenges they face in their daily lives and develop strategies to cope with them.

2) **Reducing Rumination and Avoidance:** By focusing on the present, CBT aims to reduce excessive rumination about the past and anticipatory anxiety about the future. Rumination involves getting lost in negative thoughts and dwelling on past events, while avoidance entails avoiding situations that trigger anxiety. By emphasizing the present, CBT encourages individuals to actively engage in the moment and confront current challenges rather than getting trapped in negative thought patterns or avoiding difficult situations.

3) **Utilizing Concrete and Pragmatic Techniques:** CBT focuses on practical and specific interventions that can be applied in daily life. It offers strategies such as mindfulness, problem-solving, behavior modification, etc., to help individuals cope with present difficulties. These techniques enable individuals to develop coping skills and enhance their emotional and behavioral functioning in the present.

Practical Sheet 2:

Step 1: Identification of Current Difficulties

- Become aware of the specific problems and symptoms you are currently experiencing in your daily life.
- Identify thought patterns or behaviors that contribute to these difficulties.

Example: *"I often feel overwhelmed by anxiety at work and feel unable to cope with professional demands."*

Step 2: Development of Adaptive Strategies

- Identify the CBT techniques that can help you deal with your current difficulties.
- Learn practical skills such as mindfulness, problem-solving, or modifying problematic behaviors.

Example: *"I will practice mindfulness to stay attentive and calm at work. I will also use problem-solving technique to approach difficult tasks in a structured manner."*

Step 3: Implementation in the Present

- Apply the learned strategies in your daily life.
- Actively engage in the present moment and face difficulties rather than avoiding them.

Example: Practice mindfulness at work by focusing on your breath and observing your thoughts and emotions without judgment. Apply problem-solving by identifying concrete steps to manage stressful tasks.

By following these steps of CBT, you can focus on current issues and develop practical strategies to address them. By actively engaging in the present, you can enhance your emotional well-being and overall functioning in your daily life.

3. Structured and Goal-Oriented Approach:

The structured and goal-oriented approach is one of the key features of Cognitive Behavioral Therapy (CBT). This approach is based on several psychological and therapeutic principles.

1) **The Need for Structure and Planning:** CBT recognizes the importance of clear structure and precise planning of therapy sessions. This helps establish a consistent therapeutic framework and maximize the effectiveness of the treatment. With a defined structure, therapists and patients can work systematically and organized toward therapeutic goals.

2) **Establishment of Clear Therapeutic Goals:** In CBT, the therapist and the patient collaborate to establish specific and measurable goals. These goals are typically related to the patient's current difficulties and the targeted issues for treatment. Setting clear goals helps create a

common focus and therapeutic direction, which enhances the patient's engagement and motivation.

3) **Development of a Concrete Treatment Plan:** Once the goals are defined, CBT involves the development of a concrete treatment plan. This plan may include various techniques and specific interventions tailored to the patient's needs. The treatment plan is typically based on established protocols and evidence-based interventions, contributing to therapy's effectiveness.

4) **Therapist-Patient Collaboration:** CBT relies on active collaboration between the therapist and the patient. The therapist guides the therapeutic process, provides information and techniques, and assists the patient in achieving their goals. The patient is actively involved in their own healing process, actively participating in sessions and applying acquired skills between sessions.

Step-by-Step Practical Sheet:
Step 1: Establishing Therapeutic Goals

- Work to identify specific issues you want to address.
- Define clear, measurable, and achievable goals that will help you address these issues.

Example: *"My therapeutic goal is to manage my social anxiety and develop communication skills to feel more comfortable during social interactions."*

Step 2: Treatment Plan Development

- Develop a concrete treatment plan.
- Identify specific techniques and interventions that will be used to achieve your goals.

Example: The treatment plan may include gradual exposure sessions to social situations, cognitive restructuring strategies to challenge negative thoughts, and assertive communication exercises to develop social skills.

Step 3: Implementation of the Treatment Plan

- Actively work on implementing the techniques and interventions from the treatment plan.

- Follow the specific steps outlined in the plan, fully engaging in the recommended exercises and practices.

Example: Participate in gradual exposure sessions with the support of your therapist, practice cognitive restructuring by identifying and challenging negative thoughts during social interactions, and train in assertive communication skills in real-life situations.

By following these steps of CBT, you can benefit from a structured, goal-oriented approach. The concrete treatment plan and collaboration with your therapist will allow you to work in a targeted and effective manner to address your specific challenges.

4. Learning through Experience:

CBT encourages experimentation and active learning. Patients are encouraged to test new ways of thinking and behaving in real-life situations to develop new skills and perspectives.

1.3 Why Choose Cognitive-Behavioral Therapy?

There are several reasons why cognitive-behavioral therapy is a popular and effective approach for treating psychological issues:

- **Proven Effectiveness:** CBT is supported by numerous scientific studies demonstrating its effectiveness in treating a wide range of disorders, such as anxiety, depression, eating disorders, phobias, and many others.
- **Practical and Concrete Approach:** CBT provides practical tools and techniques that can be applied directly in everyday life. Patients learn specific skills to manage their thoughts and behaviors, enabling them to actively take charge of their mental well-being.
- **Sustainability of Results:** By focusing on thought patterns and behaviors, CBT aims to bring about lasting changes. Patients acquire skills they can continue to use even after therapy ends, allowing them to maintain their well-being in the long term.

- **Adaptability:** CBT can be adapted to different issues and individuals. It can be used to treat a variety of disorders and can be tailored to the specific needs of each patient.
- **Therapist-Patient Collaboration:** CBT is a collaborative approach where the therapist and the patient work together to set goals, develop strategies, and solve problems. The patient is encouraged to be active in their own healing, promoting autonomy and empowerment.

By choosing cognitive-behavioral therapy, you are opting for a proven and practical approach to overcoming your emotional and behavioral challenges. Whether you are dealing with anxiety, depression, or other issues, CBT can provide you with the tools and skills needed to transform your life and achieve lasting well-being.

Limitations of Cognitive-Behavioral Therapy.

While cognitive-behavioral therapy (CBT) is a widely used and effective therapeutic approach, it also has some limitations. It is important to acknowledge them to maintain a balanced perspective:

1. **Limited Adaptability:** CBT was developed to address a wide range of psychological issues, but it may not be suitable for every individual or problem. Each person is unique and has different treatment needs and preferences. Therefore, it is normal for some individuals to require a different or complementary therapeutic approach to achieve the best results. For example, severe personality disorders may require more specialized and intensive approaches, such as dialectical behavior therapy (DBT) or psychodynamic therapy.

2. **Efforts and Commitment Required:** CBT involves active commitment and ongoing efforts from the patient to achieve lasting results. Maladaptive thought patterns and behaviors are often deeply ingrained and require time and practice to be modified. Therefore, it is normal for change not to happen overnight. Studies show that the patient's active involvement in therapy and the implementation of learned techniques are important factors for the success of the treatment (David et al., 2018).

3. **Limitations with Deep-Seated Issues:** CBT may have limitations when it comes to addressing deep and complex psychological issues, such as

severe personality disorders. These problems are often rooted in deep-seated thought patterns and traumas that require a more intensive and specialized therapeutic approach. Research suggests that personality disorders may require longer and more specific treatments, such as psychodynamic therapy, to achieve optimal results (Leichsenring et al., 2017).

4. **Dependency on the Therapeutic Relationship:** CBT often relies on a strong and trusting relationship between the patient and the therapist. The therapeutic alliance, which is the quality of the relationship between the patient and the therapist, has been identified as a key factor in the treatment's effectiveness (Norcross & Lambert, 2018). Therefore, if this relationship is not established or if the patient has difficulty fully engaging in the therapeutic process, results may be limited. This underscores the importance of finding a therapist with whom the patient feels comfortable and confident.

5. **Limits of Empirical Studies:** Although many studies have demonstrated the effectiveness of CBT, it is important to acknowledge that research findings may have methodological limitations. For example, some studies may be based on limited samples or may not account for the diversity of individual responses. Additionally, each individual is unique and may react differently to a given treatment based on their personal characteristics. Therefore, it is normal to consider research findings as general trends rather than absolute guarantees of therapeutic success.

6. **No Miracle Solution:** CBT, like any therapeutic approach, does not guarantee 100% positive results. Each individual and each situation is unique, and therapeutic success depends on various factors such as the patient's motivation, social support, the severity of the problem, and more. It is normal for some people to require longer-term therapy or other complementary approaches to achieve the best results in their healing journey.

These limitations do not question the overall effectiveness of CBT but rather emphasize that each therapeutic approach has its own strengths and limitations. It is also crucial to find the treatment that best suits each individual, taking into account their specific needs and situation.

The Basics of Behavioral and Cognitive Therapy

Cognitive Behavioral Therapy is based on two interconnected theoretical models: the cognitive model and the behavioral model. These two approaches complement each other to form a powerful integrated approach.

2.1 The Cognitive Model

The cognitive model focuses on the thoughts, beliefs, and interpretations we have about ourselves, others, and the world around us. It examines how these cognitive aspects influence our emotions and behaviors. Here are psychological and mental explanations about the cognitive model and how it operates:

1. Automatic Thoughts:

Automatic thoughts are spontaneous and rapid thoughts that arise in response to specific situations. They are often influenced by our thought patterns and core beliefs. These automatic thoughts can be positive, negative, or neutral, and they have a direct impact on our emotional experience. They are typically instantaneous and occur without conscious effort. They can be triggered by events, stimuli, or situations that recall past experiences or are associated with specific emotions.

For example, imagine that you are invited to give a presentation in front of a large group of people. Your automatic thoughts could be the following:

- **Positive Automatic Thought:** *"I am confident and well-prepared; I will succeed in this presentation."*
- **Negative Automatic Thought:** *"I will stutter and make mistakes; everyone will judge me and laugh at me."*
- **Neutral Automatic Thought:** *"I need to remember to speak slowly and clearly."*

These automatic thoughts can vary from person to person based on their thought patterns and core beliefs. They are often influenced by our past experiences, our perceptions of ourselves, others, and the world, as well as our expectations and concerns.

Automatic thoughts can be helpful as they allow us to quickly assess and interpret a situation. They can assist us in making quick decisions and reacting adaptively. However, when our automatic thoughts are negative, irrational, or based on dysfunctional thought patterns, they can lead to negative emotions such as sadness, anxiety, or anger, as well as maladaptive behaviors.

In cognitive-behavioral therapy, it is essential to identify automatic thoughts as they can be valuable indicators of underlying thought patterns that contribute to our emotional and behavioral difficulties. By becoming aware of our automatic thoughts, we can realistically evaluate them, challenge those that are irrational or unhelpful, and replace them with more adaptive and realistic thoughts. This helps to modify our emotional reactions and behaviors, thus promoting improved mental well-being.

2. Thought Patterns:

Thought patterns are enduring and stable patterns of thinking that influence our perception and interpretation of events. These patterns develop over time from our past experiences, upbringing, social interactions, and cultural influences. They are often deeply rooted and can be automatically activated during similar situations. They form in our cognitive and emotional development, primarily during childhood and adolescence. Early experiences and interactions with our environment, including family, peers, and teachers, play a crucial role in shaping these patterns. For example, if a child is regularly criticized or ridiculed by their parents, it can contribute to the formation of a negative self-schema. They may develop the core belief that they are incompetent or unworthy of love. This negative thought pattern can then influence their self-perception, perception of others, and the world throughout their life, leading to negative automatic thoughts in similar situations.

Here are some examples of common thought patterns:

- **Perfectionism Thought Pattern:** A person with this thought pattern has very high expectations of themselves and others. They believe that everything must be perfect, and if they don't achieve this

17

perfection, they criticize themselves harshly and may feel a sense of failure.

- **Mistrust Thought Pattern:** A person with this thought pattern tends to distrust others and believe that people have negative or manipulative intentions. They may interpret the actions of others negatively, leading to suspicion and distance in their interpersonal relationships.
- **Abandonment Thought Pattern:** A person with this thought pattern has a deep fear of being abandoned or rejected. They may have automatic thoughts such as "Everyone will eventually leave me" in situations where they feel emotionally vulnerable.

Thought patterns can influence our emotions, behaviors, and interactions with others. They can also contribute to the maintenance of psychological problems such as anxiety, depression, low self-esteem, etc.

In cognitive-behavioral therapy, the goal is to identify these maladaptive thought patterns, evaluate them realistically, and modify them if necessary. This involves challenging the fundamental beliefs underlying these patterns and replacing them with more adaptive and realistic thought patterns. This process of cognitive restructuring aims to promote more positive, constructive, and accurate thoughts, which can lead to positive changes in our emotions and behaviors.

3. Core Beliefs:

Core beliefs are deeply rooted convictions about ourselves, others, and the world around us. They are often formed early in our development and have a significant impact on our thoughts, emotions, and behaviors. They often stem from our past experiences, upbringing, social interactions, and our own interpretation of events. They can be positive, negative, or neutral and influence how we perceive and interpret incoming information.

For example, here are some common core beliefs:

1. **Positive Core Belief:** *"I am worthy of love and respect."* This positive core belief can lead a person to have self-confidence, maintain healthy relationships, and approach life's challenges with optimism.

2. **Negative Core Belief:** *"I am a failure, and I will never succeed."* This negative core belief can lead a person to constantly feel inadequate, fear failure, and avoid situations that could confirm this belief.
3. **Neutral Core Belief:** *"Life is unpredictable and can be challenging."* This neutral core belief can help a person be realistic about life's challenges, be prepared for difficulties, and develop skills to cope with them.

Core beliefs can be influenced by our early experiences, such as our relationship with our parents, interactions with others, and the messages we've received from society and culture. They can also be reinforced by our thinking patterns, automatic thoughts, and current interactions. They have a profound impact on our self-esteem, our perception of ourselves, others, and the world, as well as our emotions and behaviors. They can contribute to maintaining psychological problems such as anxiety, depression, self-esteem issues, phobias, and more.

In cognitive-behavioral therapy, it is important to explore and challenge core beliefs that are negative, irrational, or unhelpful. This involves examining the evidence that supports or refutes these beliefs, identifying cognitive biases that may influence them, and replacing them with more adaptive and realistic beliefs.

For example, a person with the negative core belief *"I am a failure, and I will never succeed"* might explore the positive experiences and accomplishments they have had in their life to challenge this belief. They could also develop a more adaptive belief such as *"I can learn from my mistakes, and I am capable of success if I commit and make an effort."*

By modifying negative or dysfunctional core beliefs, one can improve self-esteem, interpersonal relationships, self-confidence, and overall mental well-being.

The cognitive model is used to understand how our thoughts, thinking patterns, and core beliefs influence our emotions and behaviors. It emphasizes that it is not external events that directly cause our emotions but rather our interpretation of these events. Therefore, by changing our thoughts and replacing negative or irrational automatic thoughts with more adaptive and realistic ones, we can change our emotions and behavioral reactions.

In the context of cognitive-behavioral therapy, it is essential to identify automatic thoughts, which are spontaneous thoughts that arise in response to specific situations. These automatic thoughts can be positive, negative, or neutral, but they have a direct impact on our emotional experience. If we tend to have negative or irrational automatic thoughts, it can lead to negative emotions such as sadness, anxiety, or anger.

Cognitive-behavioral therapy aims to help individuals identify their negative automatic thoughts, assess their realism, and replace them with more adaptive and realistic thoughts. This process of cognitive restructuring changes the perception of oneself, others, and the world, leading to positive changes in emotions and behaviors.

2.2 The Behavioral Model

The behavioral model focuses on the observation and modification of observable behaviors. According to this model, our behaviors have a significant impact on our well-being and emotions. Behaviors can maintain psychological and emotional problems, but they can also be changed to promote positive outcomes.

The cognitive-behavioral model emphasizes the interaction between thoughts, emotions, and behaviors. In addition to automatic thoughts and thought patterns, the behavioral model examines how our behaviors influence our emotional experience and thoughts.

According to the behavioral model, our behaviors result from our thoughts and emotions, but they can also influence them. Our actions can reinforce or modify our thought patterns, beliefs, and emotions.

The behavioral model is based on the idea that changing behavior can have a positive effect on our mental well-being. For example, if a person is experiencing social anxiety, avoiding social situations may be maladaptive behavior that reinforces anxiety. By working on alternative behaviors, such as gradually exposing oneself to social situations and learning social skills, the person can reduce their anxiety and change negative thought patterns.

Key principles of the behavioral model in cognitive-behavioral therapy include:

1. **Exposure:** This involves gradually confronting feared or avoided situations to reduce anxiety and change associated thought patterns. For example, a person with a spider phobia may be exposed to images of spiders, then to real spiders in a controlled environment.
2. **Skills Acquisition:** This involves acquiring new skills to cope with challenging situations. For instance, someone with social anxiety disorders may learn communication, assertiveness, and stress management techniques to better handle social interactions.
3. **Contingency Modification:** This involves changing the consequences that reinforce or maintain undesirable behavior. For example, a person who tends to procrastinate may identify immediate rewards or avoidance associated with procrastination and find strategies to modify them.
4. **Positive Reinforcement:** This involves strengthening desired behaviors through rewards or encouragement. For instance, an individual dealing with depression may set realistic daily goals and reward themselves when achieving them.

By combining cognitive and behavioral approaches, cognitive-behavioral therapy aims to help individuals modify both their thoughts and behaviors to improve their emotional well-being. By identifying negative thought patterns, dysfunctional automatic thoughts, and maladaptive behaviors, it is possible to introduce positive changes in how we think, feel, and act.

The goal of behavioral therapy is to assist individuals in developing new, healthier, and adaptive behaviors while eliminating harmful or limiting behaviors.

2.3 The Integrated Approach.

The integrated approach, also known as the integrated cognitive-behavioral approach, combines the principles and techniques of cognitive therapy and behavioral therapy within a coherent therapeutic framework. It recognizes that thoughts, emotions, and behaviors are closely linked and interact with each other.

The integrated approach acknowledges that thoughts can influence emotions and behaviors, and that behaviors can, in turn, influence thoughts and emotions. It focuses on exploring and modifying dysfunctional thoughts and behaviors, as well as on learning adaptive skills.

This approach highlights the importance of understanding how thought patterns, automatic thoughts, core beliefs, and behaviors interact to influence our experience. It uses cognitive techniques to identify and challenge negative or irrational thoughts, as well as behavioral techniques to modify maladaptive behaviors and reinforce desired behaviors.

The integrated approach combines techniques such as:

1. **Cognitive Restructuring:** This involves identifying negative automatic thoughts, evaluating them realistically, and replacing them with more adaptive and realistic thoughts.
2. **Exposure:** This involves gradually exposing individuals to feared or avoided situations in order to reduce anxiety and modify associated thought patterns.
3. **Skills Learning:** This involves acquiring practical skills to cope with difficulties, manage emotions, and improve interpersonal relationships.
4. **Positive Reinforcement:** This involves reinforcing adaptive and positive behaviors through rewards and encouragement.

The integrated approach recognizes that each individual is unique and that a personalized approach is necessary to address their specific needs. The therapist will collaborate with the client to identify thought patterns, core beliefs, and problematic behaviors, and will work together to develop effective change strategies.

Here is a metaphor to explain the integrated approach of cognitive-behavioral therapy:

Imagine that your mind is a beautiful house with multiple rooms. Each room represents a dimension of your mental experience: your thoughts, your emotions, and your behaviors. The integrated approach is about exploring and improving each room in your house to create a harmonious environment. In the room of thoughts, we identify negative automatic thoughts that can cloud your perspective. Imagine these thoughts as dirty windows that filter the sunlight. We clean them using cognitive restructuring to remove the negative stains and replace them with clearer and more positive thoughts, allowing the light to shine through the windows.

In the room of emotions, we explore emotions that may be intense or difficult to manage. Think of these emotions as turbulent waves that can disturb your inner calm. We use behavioral techniques to help you navigate these waves, understand them, and soothe them, creating a calmer ocean within you.

Finally, in the room of behaviors, we examine actions and reactions that may be problematic. Imagine these behaviors as cluttered furniture that hinders your freedom of movement. We work together to organize the furniture, using behavioral strategies to modify maladaptive behaviors and encourage more positive and constructive behaviors.

The goal of the integrated approach is to create a harmonious mental home where thoughts, emotions, and behaviors support each other in a balanced way. By cleaning the windows of thoughts, calming the waves of emotions, and organizing the furniture of behaviors, you can live in a mental home where it is pleasant to reside, promoting your well-being and personal fulfillment.

By integrating cognitive and behavioral aspects, this approach aims to provide a comprehensive and holistic understanding of psychological issues and facilitate lasting changes in how individuals think, feel, and act.

Initial Assessment and Case Formulation

The initial assessment is a crucial step in the cognitive-behavioral therapy process. It allows the therapist to gather essential information about the patient, assess their problems, and formulate an appropriate treatment plan. This step involves two important aspects: information gathering and case formulation.

3.1 Information Gathering

Information gathering during the initial assessment involves collecting detailed data about the patient's problem, personal history, medical background, current issues, and treatment goals. This step may involve several elements, such as:

1. **History:** The therapist asks questions about the patient's personal history, family, development, education, interpersonal relationships, possible traumatic experiences, lifestyle habits, etc. The goal is to understand the factors that may have contributed to the patient's current situation.

2. **Current Symptoms and Issues:** The therapist explores the specific symptoms and problems the patient is facing, such as anxiety, depression, sleep disturbances, relationship difficulties, self-esteem issues, etc. They seek to understand how these symptoms impact the patient's daily life.

3. **Medical History:** The therapist gathers information about the patient's medical history, including physical health issues, previous medical treatments, current medications, allergies, etc. This information is important for assessing physical factors that may influence the patient's mental health.

4. **History of Previous Treatments:** The therapist explores the patient's past treatment attempts, whether it's therapy, medication, or other approaches. This helps understand what has been tried before, what has worked or not, and adapt the treatment plan accordingly.

5. **Assessment of Stress Factors:** The therapist identifies current stress factors in the patient's life, such as work-related issues, family matters, financial concerns, etc. These factors can impact mental health and must be considered in case formulation.
6. **Assessment of Resources and Strengths:** The therapist also explores the patient's resources, skills, strengths, and social support system. This helps identify the patient's assets to leverage during treatment.

This information is gathered through clinical interviews, questionnaires, assessment scales, and other standardized assessment tools. In-depth information collection allows the therapist to have a comprehensive view of the patient and their specific needs, guiding case formulation and treatment plan development.

Here's a metaphor to explain the process of information gathering during the initial assessment using the analogy of a puzzle:

Imagine the patient's understanding is a complex puzzle composed of many pieces. Each piece represents specific information about the patient, such as their personal history, symptoms, medical history, current issues, resources, etc. During information collection, the therapist acts as a passionate investigator searching for the different puzzle pieces. They carefully explore every corner of the puzzle to find the missing pieces and fit them together to form a complete picture.

The therapist starts by asking questions about the patient's personal history, as if they are gathering pieces from the past to understand how they fit together and influence the current situation. Next, they focus on the current symptoms and issues, which are like central puzzle pieces, revealing the challenges the patient is facing. Simultaneously, the therapist explores the patient's medical history, which is another crucial piece of the puzzle. They seek to understand if certain physical issues may contribute to mental difficulties. Additionally, the therapist examines previous treatments, stress factors, and the patient's resources, all of which are important pieces to complete the overall puzzle picture.

Using assessment tools, clinical interviews, and other techniques, the therapist gradually gathers the puzzle pieces and meticulously adjusts them to form a coherent and understandable picture of the patient. Each collected piece is valuable information that adds to the overall view of the patient and guides the case formulation. Information gathering during the initial assessment is comparable to assembling a complex puzzle. The therapist explores each piece, each detail, and carefully puts them together to form a complete picture of the patient. It is this complete picture that will serve as the foundation for developing a personalized and effective treatment plan, enabling the resolution of the patient's difficulties in a holistic and informed manner.

Here's a concrete example to illustrate the process of information gathering during the initial assessment:

Suppose an individual seeks help for symptoms of generalized anxiety. The therapist begins by asking questions to gather detailed information about the person's situation:

1. **History:** The therapist asks the individual to recount their personal history, including their development, education, family, and relationships. It is discovered that the person experienced stressful childhood experiences, which may contribute to their current anxiety.
2. **Current Symptoms and Issues:** The therapist explores the individual's specific symptoms, such as anxious thoughts, physical sensations of anxiety, difficulties with concentration, and excessive worries. It is revealed that anxiety significantly impacts the person's daily activities and quality of life.
3. **Medical History:** The therapist requests information about the individual's medical history. It is found that the person has a medical condition that can exacerbate anxiety symptoms. This indicates

that an integrated approach, considering medical aspects, may be beneficial.

4. **Past Treatment History:** The therapist inquires if the person has previously received treatment for anxiety. The individual mentions trying medications but not experiencing lasting effects. This suggests that other therapeutic approaches may be explored.

5. **Assessment of Stress Factors:** The therapist explores the individual's current stress factors. The person mentions work-related issues, relationship difficulties, and financial concerns. These stress factors can contribute to anxiety and need to be considered in treatment.

6. **Assessment of Resources and Strengths:** The therapist seeks to identify the individual's resources and strengths. The person mentions stress management skills and support from their immediate family. These resources can be utilized in treatment to help the individual cope with anxiety.

Using this information, the therapist develops an overall understanding of the individual's situation. They identify negative thought patterns, core beliefs, and emotional reactions that contribute to the person's anxiety. This understanding guides the case formulation and the development of a tailored treatment plan, which may include cognitive interventions to challenge anxious thoughts, relaxation techniques to manage physical sensations of anxiety, and strategies for coping with specific stressors.

This example illustrates how in-depth information gathering during the initial assessment provides a comprehensive view of the individual's difficulties, helping steer the therapeutic process and customize the treatment approach.

In the case of self-therapy:
In the context of self-therapy, information gathering is done independently by the individual. This can involve introspective processes where the person seeks to understand their own thoughts, emotions, behaviors, and thought

patterns. Here are some approaches one can adopt for information gathering during self-therapy:

- **Journaling:** Keeping a journal can be a powerful way to gather information about oneself. Regularly writing down one's thoughts, emotions, reactions to specific situations, recurring thought patterns, achievements, and challenges can help gain a better understanding of one's own cognitive and behavioral patterns.
- **Self-observation:** Being mindful of oneself and observing emotional reactions, automatic thoughts, and behaviors in different situations can provide insights into underlying thought patterns. Mentally or in writing, noting observations can be helpful in gaining perspective and analyzing reactions.
- **Symptom Evaluation:** Using online assessment questionnaires or self-assessment tools to measure one's symptoms can provide a more objective understanding of one's emotional and mental state. There are many online resources that offer self-assessment questionnaires for specific conditions such as anxiety, depression, and more.
- **Research and Learning:** Conducting research on cognitive-behavioral therapy theories and concepts can help gain knowledge about thought patterns, cognitive restructuring techniques, adaptive behaviors, and more. This knowledge can serve as a foundation for a better understanding of one's own mental and emotional processes.

Here's a concrete example of information gathering during the initial assessment: Let's say you are embarking on self-therapy to work on your self-esteem. You can follow the steps below to collect relevant information:

1. **Self-Observation:** Take the time to observe your thoughts, emotions, and behaviors related to self-esteem. Note the moments when you criticize yourself, experience low self-esteem, or struggle to accept compliments. For example: You notice that every time you make a mistake or don't meet the expectations you've set for yourself, you harshly criticize yourself and say things like *"I'm so stupid"* or *"I'm never good enough."* You record these moments when you self-criticize and how it affects your mood and confidence.

2. **Reflection on Personal History:** Think about past experiences that may have influenced your self-esteem. Identify moments when you may have received negative or critical messages from others or if events had an impact on your self-confidence. For example: You remember an experience from your adolescence where you were bullied at school. The negative comments and constant criticism affected your self-esteem and cast doubt on your abilities and self-worth.

3. **Analysis of Automatic Thoughts:** Identify the negative automatic thoughts that arise when you evaluate yourself or when you face situations that challenge your self-esteem. Note these thoughts and try to understand the recurring thought patterns that contribute to low self-esteem. For example: When you are faced with a situation where you have to speak in public, you notice that negative automatic thoughts emerge, such as *"Others will judge me"* or *"I will make a mistake, and everyone will see it."* You record these thoughts and realize that they contribute to low self-esteem and social anxiety.

4. **Evaluation of Behaviors:** Observe how your self-esteem affects your behaviors. For example, notice if you avoid certain situations or engage in perfectionistic behaviors to try to compensate for low self-esteem. For instance: You avoid group meetings at work and shy away from significant social interactions, limiting your opportunities for personal and professional growth.

5. **Identification of External Influences:** Reflect on the influence of your social and cultural environment on your self-esteem. Consider social norms, family expectations, toxic relationships, or constant comparisons to others. For example: You think about social norms and family expectations that may influence your self-esteem. You realize that your family has always valued academic and professional success, creating constant pressure to be perfect and succeed in everything you undertake.

6. **Recognition of Resources :** Identify internal and external resources that can support your self-esteem. This may include your skills, past accomplishments, the support of close friends or mentors, or

activities that bring you satisfaction. For example: You identify that you have a trusted friend with whom you can share your feelings and concerns, and who supports you unconditionally. You also note that you have developed skills and achievements in your career that demonstrate your worth and abilities.

By gathering this information, you can begin to develop a clearer picture of your self-esteem and the factors influencing your self-confidence. This understanding can serve as a foundation for developing self-therapy strategies, such as cognitive restructuring to challenge negative thoughts, behavioral experimentation to strengthen your self-esteem, and exploring new activities that promote a better self-image.

In the case of self-therapy, it's important to recognize that the support of a qualified mental health professional can be beneficial in guiding the therapeutic process. A professional can provide external perspectives, advice, and personalized strategies that can facilitate the healing process. If possible, it is recommended to consult with a professional for additional and informed support.

3.2 Developing the Case Formulation

Developing the case formulation is a key step in cognitive-behavioral therapy (CBT) that involves integrating the information gathered during the assessment to form a comprehensive understanding of the case. The case formulation helps identify thought patterns, core beliefs, automatic thoughts, emotions, and behaviors that contribute to the individual's difficulties. Here are the general steps in developing the case formulation in CBT:

1. **Information Synthesis:** The therapist reviews the data collected during the assessment, including information gathered during interviews, questionnaire and assessment results, observations, and medical and psychological history. They look for recurring themes and patterns in this information.

2. **Identification of Thought Patterns and Core Beliefs:** The therapist identifies thought patterns and core beliefs that appear to play a central

role in the individual's difficulties. These patterns can be negative, irrational, or dysfunctional and may contribute to negative emotions and problematic behaviors.

3. **Hypothetical Formulation:** The therapist develops a hypothetical case formulation, which is a coherent description of interconnected thought patterns, core beliefs, automatic thoughts, emotions, and behaviors. This formulation highlights the relationships between these different elements and explains how they reinforce each other.

4. **Validation of Formulation with the Individual:** The therapist shares the hypothetical formulation with the individual and discusses it together. This is a collaborative step where the individual is invited to provide additional information, validate, or clarify aspects of the formulation. This step aims to achieve shared understanding and strengthen therapeutic collaboration.

5. **Using the Formulation to Guide Treatment:** The case formulation is used as a guide to develop a personalized treatment plan for the individual. It helps the therapist select appropriate cognitive and behavioral interventions to target identified thought patterns, core beliefs, negative emotions, and problematic behaviors.

CBT case formulation provides an overview of the individual's difficulties, focusing on the cognitive and behavioral processes contributing to their problems. It provides a solid foundation for customizing treatment and guiding specific interventions.

Here's a concrete example to illustrate the development of a case formulation: Suppose you are seeing a therapist for symptoms of depression. Here's how the therapist could formulate your case:

1. **Identification of Thought Patterns:** The therapist notices that you have negative thought patterns such as rumination, pessimistic thinking, and self-deprecation. For instance, you tend to dwell on past failures, constantly criticize yourself, and anticipate the worst in situations.

2. **Exploration of Core Beliefs:** The therapist explores your core beliefs about yourself, others, and the world. They discover that you have an underlying belief that you are inherently unworthy of love and happiness, and that others are invariably judgmental and hostile. These beliefs influence your self-esteem and your perception of social relationships.
3. **Analysis of Automatic Thoughts:** The therapist identifies negative automatic thoughts that arise when you're feeling depressed. For example, when you experience a minor disappointment, you automatically think, "I'm a total failure" or "Everything is my fault." These automatic thoughts reinforce your depression and amplify negative emotions.
4. **Assessment of Emotions:** The therapist examines the emotions accompanying your depression, such as sadness, loss of interest, fatigue, and irritability. They observe how these emotions affect your behaviors, such as reduced engagement in activities, social withdrawal, and sleep disturbances.

By integrating this information, the therapist can formulate your case as follows:

"The primary issue is depression, which is influenced by negative thought patterns such as rumination, pessimistic thinking, and self-deprecation. These thought patterns are fueled by underlying core beliefs that I am inherently unworthy of love and happiness, and that others are judgmental and hostile. These negative automatic thoughts arise in response to situations of disappointment and reinforce depression. This manifests as emotions like sadness, loss of interest, fatigue, and irritability, leading to reduced engagement in activities, social withdrawal, and sleep disturbances."

This case formulation allows the therapist to understand the interconnected thought patterns, core beliefs, automatic thoughts, emotions, and behaviors contributing to your depression. Based on this understanding, the therapist can develop a personalized treatment plan that includes cognitive interventions to challenge negative thought patterns, behavioral strategies to increase engagement in enjoyable activities, and belief adjustment techniques to modify underlying beliefs.

In the case of self-therapy:

Suppose you want to work on your social anxiety, which arises when you are in the presence of new people or in social situations. Here's how you can formulate your case:

1. **Identification of Thought Patterns:** You realize that you have negative thought patterns contributing to your social anxiety. For example, you tend to believe that others are constantly judging you or that you must be perfect to be accepted. These thought patterns reinforce your social anxiety and lead you to avoid social situations.

2. **Exploration of Core Beliefs:** You reflect on the core beliefs underpinning your social anxiety. For instance, you may believe that your self-worth depends on others' approval or that you must be liked by everyone to feel good about yourself. These beliefs influence your self-perception and how you view others in social situations.

3. **Analysis of Automatic Thoughts:** You identify negative automatic thoughts that arise when you confront a social situation. For example, when you enter a room filled with unfamiliar people, you automatically think, "They will all judge me and find me boring." These automatic thoughts amplify your social anxiety and may lead to avoidance.

4. **Assessment of Emotions:** You acknowledge the emotions accompanying your social anxiety, such as nervousness, fear of rejection, or discomfort. You also note how these emotions impact your behaviors, such as avoiding social gatherings or remaining silent during conversations.

By integrating these different pieces of information, you can formulate your case as follows:

"My primary challenge is social anxiety, which is fueled by negative thought patterns like constant judgment from others and the need for perfection. These thought patterns are rooted in core beliefs that my self-worth depends

on others' approval and that I must be universally liked to feel good about myself. These negative automatic thoughts arise in response to social situations and intensify my social anxiety. This results in emotions like nervousness, fear of rejection, and discomfort, leading to avoidance of social interactions or staying silent in conversations."

This case formulation gives you a comprehensive understanding of your social anxiety difficulties and highlights the interconnectedness of thought patterns, core beliefs, automatic thoughts, emotions, and behaviors. Based on this understanding, you can consider specific self-therapy strategies to challenge negative thought patterns, modify underlying beliefs, and develop social skills to better manage your anxiety in social situations.

A strong case formulation provides a foundation for an individualized and effective treatment plan. It guides the selection of specific interventions, therapeutic goals, and follow-up strategies. Case formulation is also a valuable tool for establishing a common understanding between the therapist and the patient, promoting collaboration, and engagement in the therapeutic process.

Cognitive Techniques

Cognitive techniques are a central element of cognitive-behavioral therapy. They aim to identify, assess, and modify negative or irrational automatic thoughts that contribute to problematic emotions and behaviors. Here are some commonly used cognitive techniques:

4.1 Identification of Automatic Thoughts

Identifying automatic thoughts involves becoming aware of thoughts that spontaneously arise in response to a given situation. These thoughts can be positive, negative, or neutral. In the context of CBT, the focus is primarily on negative automatic thoughts that contribute to negative emotions.

The therapist encourages the patient to observe and record their automatic thoughts in specific situations. This can be done using a thought journal or thought recording. The goal is to become aware of recurring thought patterns and begin examining them objectively.

Example of a situation: You received negative feedback on a project you presented during a work meeting. You feel devalued and think you are a total failure.

- **Identification of Automatic Thoughts:** Take a moment to note your automatic thoughts in this situation:
- **Automatic Thoughts:** "I am a total failure, "No one takes me seriously, "I am not competent."

Practical Sheet - Identification of Automatic Thoughts:

1. Identify the specific situation where you experience negative emotions.
2. Note the automatic thoughts that come to your mind in this situation.
3. Be aware of recurring thought patterns or common themes.

4.2 Evaluation of Automatic Thoughts

Once automatic thoughts have been identified, it is important to evaluate them realistically. The task involves examining the validity and accuracy of negative automatic thoughts. Often, these thoughts are based on cognitive distortions, reasoning errors, or negative interpretations of oneself, others, or the world.

The therapist assists the patient in challenging their automatic thoughts by seeking evidence for and against these thoughts. Questions such as "What evidence supports this thought?" or "Is there any evidence that contradicts it?" are asked to help objectively evaluate automatic thoughts.

For example: Now, examine the automatic thoughts and evaluate them realistically by looking for evidence for and against these thoughts:

- **Evidence For:** The negative feedback was specific to this project; I can learn from this experience.
- **Evidence Against:** I have received compliments for my work in the past; I have skills and knowledge in my field.

Practical Sheet - Evaluation of Automatic Thoughts:

- Take a negative automatic thought you have identified.
- Look for evidence to support this thought.
- Look for evidence that contradicts this thought.
- Objectively evaluate the evidence and judge if the thought is realistic and justified.

4.3 Cognitive Restructuring

Cognitive restructuring aims to replace negative automatic thoughts with more adaptive and realistic thoughts. It is an active process of reshaping thought patterns to promote positive emotions and healthy behaviors.

The therapist helps the patient examine contradictory or alternative evidence to their negative automatic thoughts. Techniques such as reframing, evidence gathering, relabeling, or using positive affirmations are used to assist the patient in developing new perspectives and ways of thinking.

For example: Now, replace negative automatic thoughts with more adaptive and realistic thoughts:

- **Restructured Thoughts:** *"The negative feedback was specific to this project and does not question my overall skills,"I have received compliments in the past; I can learn from this experience and improve."*

Practical Sheet - Cognitive Restructuring:
1. Take a negative automatic thought you want to restructure.
2. Identify contradictory or alternative evidence to this thought.
3. Rephrase the automatic thought into a more adaptive and realistic thought.
4. Regularly repeat the new thoughts to reinforce them.

4.4 Problem-Solving Skills Training

Problem-Solving Skills Training is a cognitive technique aimed at helping patients develop practical skills to cope with everyday life difficulties. This technique involves identifying specific problems the patient is facing, generating alternative solutions, evaluating the pros and cons of each solution, and implementing the best one.

For example: To deal with this situation, you can use Problem-Solving Skills Training:

- **Identify the problem:** Receiving a negative comment on the project.
- **Generate alternative solutions:** Seek feedback, improve the project, or discuss the issue with colleagues.
- **Evaluate the pros and cons of each solution:** Consider the effectiveness, feasibility, and potential outcomes of each approach.

- **Implement the best solution:** Take action based on the chosen approach and monitor the results.

Practical Sheet - Problem-Solving Skills Training:
1. Identify a specific problem you want to solve.
2. Generate multiple alternative solutions.
3. Evaluate the advantages and disadvantages of each solution.
4. Implement the best solution and assess the results.

By using these cognitive techniques and practicing regularly, you can gradually develop a more realistic and positive perspective, challenge negative automatic thoughts, and adopt more adaptive and realistic thoughts.

These cognitive techniques are powerful tools used in cognitive-behavioral therapy to help individuals recognize and modify their negative thought patterns. By identifying automatic thoughts, realistically evaluating them, restructuring them, and developing problem-solving skills, patients can gain a more positive and realistic perspective, leading to healthier emotions and more adaptive behaviors.

Behavioral Techniques

Behavioral techniques are another essential aspect of cognitive-behavioral therapy. They aim to modify problematic behaviors and promote healthier and more adaptive behaviors. Here are some commonly used behavioral techniques:

5.1 Exposure and Response Prevention

Exposure and Response Prevention (ERP) is a commonly used technique in cognitive-behavioral therapy to treat anxiety disorders such as phobias, obsessive-compulsive disorder (OCD), and post-traumatic stress disorder (PTSD). The goal of this technique is to help individuals confront their fears and reduce their anxiety by gradually exposing themselves to feared situations and preventing avoidance behaviors.

Here is a concrete example of using exposure and response prevention:

Example Situation: You have a phobia of spiders that limits your daily life. You are so afraid of spiders that you panic and go to great lengths to avoid them.

1. **Establishment of a Fear Hierarchy:** You and your therapist create a hierarchical list of situations related to your fear of spiders, starting with those that cause mild anxiety and progressing to those that trigger more intense anxiety. For example:
   - Looking at a picture of a spider
   - Watching a video of a spider
   - Observing a spider in a container
   - Being in the same room as a spider
   - Holding a spider in your hand
2. **Gradual Exposure:** You begin by exposing yourself to the least anxiety-provoking situation in your hierarchy, such as looking at a picture of a spider, while intentionally confronting your anxiety

instead of avoiding it. You repeat this exposure regularly until your anxiety significantly decreases.

3. **Response Prevention:** During exposure, you prevent any avoidance or safety behaviors that could reinforce your fear. For example, you refrain from checking if a spider is actually in the room, asking someone to kill it for you, or fleeing to avoid the situation. You learn to tolerate discomfort and realize that your fear will naturally diminish over time.

4. **Progression in the Hierarchy:** Once you feel comfortable with one exposure step, you move on to the next one in your hierarchy, gradually increasing the difficulty of the exposed situations. You continue to expose yourself and prevent avoidance behaviors until you can face more anxiety-provoking situations without experiencing excessive anxiety.

5. **Progress Consolidation:** Over time, you notice that your anxiety gradually decreases as you expose yourself and prevent avoidance behaviors. You gain confidence in your ability to confront your fear of spiders and lead a more functional and fulfilling life.

Exposure and Response Prevention typically require the guidance and support of a qualified mental health professional to ensure that the progression is appropriate and safe. However, it's important to note that this example is purely illustrative and does not replace supervised therapy.

5.2 Behavioral Activation.

Behavioral activation is a technique used in cognitive-behavioral therapy to treat depression and other mood disorders. The goal of this technique is to stimulate enjoyable and rewarding behaviors to combat the apathy and inactivity often associated with depression.

Here is a concrete example of using behavioral activation:

Example Situation: You have been feeling depressed for some time and have lost interest in activities you used to enjoy, such as going out with friends, exercising, or pursuing hobbies.

1. **Identification of Pleasant Activities:** Make a list of activities that have brought you pleasure in the past, even if they don't seem appealing to you right now. This can include simple things like taking a walk, listening to a relaxing podcast, reading a book, cooking, etc.

2. **Establishment of an Activity Schedule:** Create a weekly schedule and plan specific times for the enjoyable activities you have identified. Try to choose at least one activity per day, even if you don't feel like it. The goal is to gradually reintroduce pleasant activities into your routine.

3. **Taking Action:** Actively engage in the planned activities, even if you don't initially feel enthusiastic. Force yourself to participate, keeping in mind that it is part of the depression treatment process.

4. **Emotion and Gratification Notation:** After each activity, note the emotions you have felt and the rewarding moments you have experienced. This can help you become aware of the small pleasures and moments of satisfaction you might have missed if you had remained inactive.

5. **Reevaluation and Adjustment:** Over time, reassess your activities and adjust your schedule based on your changing preferences. Don't hesitate to try new activities to broaden your horizons and discover new sources of pleasure.

By practicing behavioral activation, you can gradually break the cycle of inactivity and depression by reintroducing enjoyable activities into your life. This can help you regain a sense of satisfaction, boost your self-esteem, and improve your overall mood.

5.3 Relaxation Techniques

Relaxation techniques are effective tools for reducing stress, anxiety, and promoting a state of calm and relaxation. They are used in various therapeutic approaches, including cognitive-behavioral therapy, to help individuals manage their emotions and physical reactions to stress. Here are some of the most commonly used relaxation techniques:

1. **Deep Breathing:** Take a few moments to sit comfortably, close your eyes, and focus on your breathing. Inhale deeply through your nose, expanding your abdomen, then exhale slowly through your mouth. Repeat this process several times while concentrating on your breath, which can help calm the nervous system and reduce feelings of anxiety. Here's how to practice it:
   - Find a quiet place where you can sit comfortably.
   - Close your eyes and focus on your breathing.
   - Take a deep breath in through your nose, counting to four, feeling your abdomen rise.
   - Briefly hold your breath for a count of four.
   - Exhale slowly through your mouth for a count of four, feeling your abdomen deflate.
   - Repeat this deep breathing process for a few minutes, focusing on the regular rhythm of your breath and letting distracting thoughts pass without attaching to them.

2. **Progressive Muscle Relaxation:** Begin by lying down or sitting comfortably. Tense the muscles in one part of your body, such as your arms, and then completely release them while focusing on the sensations of relaxation. Move on to another part of the body, like the legs, and repeat the process until you have relaxed all muscle groups. This technique can help release bodily tension and promote an overall sense of relaxation. Here's how to practice it:
   - Lie down or sit comfortably.
   - Begin with the muscles in your feet. Tighten them by contracting the muscles for a few seconds, then completely release them while feeling the relaxation spread.
   - Gradually move up your body, contracting and releasing each muscle group, from your legs to your head.
   - Take your time to feel the relaxation and comfort at each step.

- Pay attention to the sensations of relaxation and lightness in the muscles as you release them.

3. **Guided Visualization:** Imagine yourself in a calm and peaceful place, like a beach or a garden. Visualize the details of this place, the colors, sounds, and sensations. Mentally immerse yourself in this relaxing environment and let your imagination create a soothing experience. This technique can help distract from stress and induce a state of deep relaxation. Here's how to practice it:
   - Sit comfortably or lie down in a quiet place.
   - Close your eyes and begin to imagine a peaceful and relaxing place, like a beach or a garden.
   - Visualize the details of this place, the colors, shapes, sounds, and sensations.
   - Try to fully immerse yourself in this mental experience using all your senses.
   - Stay in this guided visualization state for as long as you wish, focusing on the sensations of calm and relaxation.

4. **Mindfulness Meditation:** Sit comfortably and pay attention to the present moment, without judging the thoughts or sensations that arise. Let thoughts pass without attaching to them, focusing on your breath or bodily sensations. Mindfulness meditation can help cultivate a state of calm and presence, reducing mental rumination and promoting relaxation. Here's how to practice it:
   - Sit in a comfortable position, with your feet flat on the floor and your hands resting on your knees.
   - Close your eyes and focus on your breath. Notice the movement of the air entering and leaving your body.
   - Let thoughts come and go without attaching to them, simply observing them without judgment.
   - Pay attention to your bodily sensations, such as the sensations of contact with the chair, sensations of tension or relaxation in different parts of the body.

- If your mind drifts away from the present moment, gently bring your attention back to your breath or bodily sensations.

It is important to note that everyone may have different preferences when it comes to relaxation techniques. It can be helpful to experiment with different methods to find the ones that work best for you. Furthermore, regular practice of relaxation techniques is generally recommended to fully reap the benefits.

5.4 Social Skills Training

Social skills training is a technique used in cognitive-behavioral therapy to help individuals improve their social interactions and relational skills. This can be particularly beneficial for people who struggle to establish social connections, communicate effectively, or handle difficult social situations. Here's a practical guide to implementing this technique:

1. **Identification of Social Skills to Develop:** Think about the areas in which you want to improve your social skills. This may include skills such as active listening, non-verbal communication, conflict management, social stress management, etc. Choose one or two specific skills to focus on initially.

2. **Observation and Learning:** Observe people who are socially adept and possess the skills you want to develop. Take note of their behaviors, facial expressions, tone of voice, and communication style. This can be done in real-life situations or through media such as videos or films.

3. **Practice of Social Skills:** Identify situations in which you can practice your social skills. Start with simple and less intimidating situations, then progress to more complex ones as you gain confidence. Put yourself in the situation and actively engage in using the social skills you want to develop. For example, if you're working on active listening, focus on attentive listening, maintaining eye contact, paraphrasing information, etc.

4. **Debriefing:** After each social interaction, take the time to reflect on your performance. Identify aspects you handled well and areas where you can improve. Be kind to yourself and acknowledge the progress you've

made. Use the experiences to adjust your approach and continue practicing and developing your social skills.

5. **Progressive Training:** Once you feel comfortable with one social skill, move on to another and continue training progressively. Add more complex and challenging situations as you progress.

6. **Support and Additional Resources:** If you struggle to develop your social skills independently, consider seeking support groups or workshops that focus on social skills development. You can also consult a mental health professional specialized in social therapy for more targeted guidance.

Behavioral techniques are practical and effective tools used in cognitive-behavioral therapy to help individuals modify problematic behaviors, develop new skills, and improve their emotional well-being. Whether through exposure and response prevention, behavioral activation, relaxation techniques, or social skills training, these techniques provide concrete ways to promote positive changes in behavior and foster better social and emotional adaptation.

Here is a list of social skills you can train:

1. **Verbal Communication:**

+ **Active Listening:**
  - **Example exercise:** Choose a partner and take a few minutes to discuss a given topic (e.g., your last trip). During the conversation, practice active listening using the following strategies:
    - ✓ Ask open-ended questions such as "What places did you visit?" or "What did you enjoy the most about your trip?"
    - ✓ Provide periodic summaries by recapping the main points discussed by your partner.
    - ✓ Show interest by making positive comments such as "That sounds like an incredible experience!" or nodding to encourage your partner to continue.
    - ✓ Avoid interruptions and let your partner finish their sentences without interrupting them.

- **Clear Expression:**
  - **Example Exercise:** Choose a specific topic or situation and prepare a short presentation on that topic. Practice expressing your ideas in a concise and clear manner, using simple sentences and avoiding excessive information or digressions. Train yourself to convey your message clearly and understandably to your audience.

    For example: Topic: My summer vacation. Presentation: *"During my summer vacation, I spent two weeks at the beach with my family. We enjoyed the sun, swam in the sea, and took long walks on the sand. It was relaxing and enjoyable to spend time together away from the daily stress."* In this example, the goal is to present the main information about the summer vacation in a concise and clear manner. The focus is on the highlights and activities, while avoiding excessive details. By practicing this type of exercise, you can improve your ability to convey your ideas concisely and comprehensibly.

- **Empathy:**
  - **Example exercise:** Choose a partner and discuss an emotionally charged personal experience. During the conversation, practice empathy using the following techniques:
    - ✓ Practice active listening by being attentive to their emotions and concerns.
    - ✓ Validate their emotions using phrases such as "I understand this may be difficult for you" or "I can see that it makes you sad."
    - ✓ Show your support by offering words of encouragement and expressing your availability to help if needed.

The goal of these exercises is to develop your skills in verbal communication by focusing on active listening, clear expression, and empathy. By regularly practicing these skills, you can improve your interactions with others, promote better mutual understanding, and strengthen your interpersonal relationships.

2. Non-verbal communication:

Non-verbal communication plays an essential role in our daily interactions. It complements verbal language by conveying subtle information, such as emotions, engagement, and interest. Here are some key elements of non-verbal communication and practical tips for implementing them:

Body Language:

- ✓ **Use Gestures:** Gestures can reinforce the verbal message and add clarity to communication. For example, use hand gestures to illustrate a point or show the extent of something.
- ✓ **Adopt an Open Posture:** An open posture, with uncrossed arms and a slight lean towards the person you are communicating with, signals openness, attentiveness, and engagement in the interaction.

Eye Contact:

- ✓ **Establish Eye Contact:** Establishing appropriate eye contact with your conversation partner is essential to demonstrate your interest and active listening. Directly looking into the other person's eyes strengthens the connection and mutual understanding.
- ✓ **Maintain Eye Contact:** During the conversation, regularly maintain eye contact to demonstrate your engagement and presence. However, avoid overly intense eye contact, which could be perceived as intrusive.

Facial Expressions:

- ✓ **Use Appropriate Facial Expressions:** Facial expressions convey emotions and intentions. Try to match your facial expressions to your message. For example, smile when you're happy or interested, and adopt a more serious expression during serious or grave discussions.
- ✓ **Be Mindful of Your Facial Expression:** Ensure that your facial expression is consistent with the message you want to convey. Sometimes, contradictory facial expressions can lead to confusion or misinterpretation of your communication.

It is important to note that non-verbal communication can vary depending on culture, individual, and context. Therefore, it is essential to observe and adapt to the specific non-verbal norms and signals of each situation.

By practicing effective non-verbal communication, you can strengthen your interactions, improve mutual understanding, and build deeper connections with others. Be mindful of your body language, eye contact, and facial expressions, and adapt them to the needs of each situation.

3. Social Problem Solving:

- **Conflict Resolution Skills:** Identify sources of conflict, seek mutually beneficial solutions, and negotiate compromises to resolve disputes.

Here is a practical sheet with an example for conflict resolution skills:

1. Identify the sources of conflict:

Example: Imagine a situation where you and your colleague have differing opinions on how to organize a team meeting. Take the time to identify the various sources of conflict, such as differences in priorities, working styles, or personal preferences.

2. Seek mutually beneficial solutions:

Example: In the team meeting situation, discuss with your colleague to find solutions that meet the needs of both parties. For example, you could propose dividing the meeting into two parts, incorporating each other's top priorities into the agenda.

3. Negotiate compromises:

Example: If you and your colleague are unable to reach a full agreement, look for compromises that allow each party to make concessions while achieving a satisfactory outcome. For example, you could agree to adopt certain elements of your colleague's approach while ensuring that your priorities are also taken into account.

The goal of these examples is to illustrate how to apply conflict resolution skills in a concrete situation. By identifying sources of conflict, seeking mutually beneficial solutions, and negotiating compromises, you can achieve a satisfactory resolution and maintain harmonious relationships with others.

↓ Assertiveness Skills:

Being assertive means being able to express your needs, opinions, and boundaries clearly, respectfully, and effectively. It also involves recognizing and respecting the needs and rights of others.

Here is a step-by-step guide to developing assertiveness skills:

- **Step 1: Identifying Needs, Opinions, and Boundaries.**

Take the time to reflect on your needs, opinions, and boundaries regarding a specific situation. For example, you could identify the need for personal time, the opinion that your contribution is important, or the boundary of not accepting constant interruptions in your work.

- **Step 2: Clarity and Specificity**

Express your needs, opinions, and boundaries clearly and specifically. Avoid generalities and be precise in your communication. For example, instead of saying "I want more free time," you could say "I need two hours a day to relax and recharge."

- **Step 3: Mutual Respect**

Ensure that your communication respects the needs and rights of others. Avoid imposing your needs on others and seek solutions that take into account all the interests involved. For example, if you need time for yourself, propose a solution that also allows the other person to meet their needs, such as finding a time slot that works for both.

- **Step 4: Use of "I" and Assertiveness**

Use sentences starting with "I" to express your needs, opinions, and boundaries. This empowers your communication and avoids blaming or criticizing others. For example, say *"I feel the need to share my opinion on this matter"* rather than *"You never listen to me."*

- **Step 5: Non-Verbal Communication**

Ensure that your body language and tone of voice reflect your assertiveness. Maintain an upright posture, maintain appropriate eye contact, and use a calm and confident tone of voice.

- **Step 6: Training and Practice**

Assertiveness is a skill that improves with practice. Look for opportunities to train yourself to be assertive in real-life situations. Start with less stressful situations and progress to more complex ones as you gain confidence.

For example, let's imagine that you need more time for yourself in the evening after work. Here's how you could apply the steps:

- **Step 1:** Identify your need: you need time to relax and recharge after a day of work.
- **Step 2:** Be clear and specific: express that you need 30 minutes of quiet time each evening to relax.
- **Step 3:** Mutual respect: propose a solution that also respects the needs of your partner or family, such as agreeing on a time slot where you can have your quiet time without disrupting the activities of others.
- **Step 4:** Use assertiveness: say "I need 30 minutes of quiet time every evening to relax and recharge. Would it be possible to find a time that works for everyone?"
- **Step 5:** Ensure that your non-verbal communication is aligned with your message. Maintain eye contact, an open posture, and use a confident tone of voice. Step 6: Practice this assertive communication regularly to strengthen your assertiveness skills.

By developing your assertiveness skills, you will be able to communicate your needs, opinions, and boundaries in a respectful and effective manner, while promoting balanced and satisfying relationships with others.

↓ Handling Criticism:

Accept constructive criticism non-defensively, acknowledging learning opportunities and avoiding impulsive or aggressive reactions.

Fact Sheet: Handling Criticism

Handling criticism is a valuable skill that allows you to accept constructive criticism non-defensively and turn these comments into learning opportunities. Here is a step-by-step guide to develop this skill:

- **Step 1: Receive criticism without reacting impulsively**

When you receive criticism, take a mental pause to avoid reacting immediately in a defensive or aggressive manner. Take a deep breath and take a moment to reflect before responding. **For example:** A colleague points out that you could improve your organization during team meetings.

- **Step 2: Actively listen and remain open**

Listen carefully to the criticism without interrupting. Be open to the other person's perspective and be willing to understand their point of view. **For example:** Listen attentively to your colleague's suggestions on meeting organization and try to understand why they believe improvements could be made.

- **Step 3: Recognize learning opportunities**

View criticism as an opportunity to learn and grow. Recognize that even constructive criticism can help you improve and develop new skills. **For example:** Accept that you could benefit from better meeting organization to increase efficiency and productivity.

- **Step 4: Ask clarifying questions**

If you need more details or clarification on the criticism, feel free to ask respectful questions to better understand the other person's expectations and suggestions. **For example:** Ask your colleague which specific aspects of meeting organization they think you could improve.

- **Step 5: Responding constructively**

Once you have taken the time to listen and understand the criticism, respond in a constructive and respectful manner. Explain how you intend to use this feedback to improve. **For example:** Respond to your colleague by saying, "Thank you for your feedback. I will take your suggestions into account and work on better meeting organization in the future. I appreciate your input to make our team more effective."

- **Step 6: Follow up and implement changes**

Make sure to follow up on how you are using the feedback to bring about positive changes. Show that you have learned from the criticism by implementing concrete actions. **For example:** In the upcoming meetings, apply your colleague's suggestions by adopting a more organized approach and encouraging the participation of all team members.

By developing skills in handling criticism, you will be able to accept constructive feedback non-defensively and leverage it for self-improvement. An open and receptive attitude will enable you to turn criticisms into learning opportunities and strengthen your professional and personal skills.

4. Interpersonal Skills:

⊥ Building and Maintaining Friendships:

Initiating and nurturing friendly relationships, showing interest and commitment to others, and maintaining regular communication.

Practical Sheet: Building and Maintaining Friendships

Interpersonal skills are essential for developing and maintaining healthy friendships. Here is a step-by-step guide to develop these skills:

- **Step 1: Initiating Friendly Relationships**

Show Interest in Others : Ask open-ended questions to learn more about people and their lives. Show genuine interest in what they have to say. Example: When meeting someone for the first time, ask them to tell you about their interests or passions.

- **Step 2: Establish Regular Communication**

Maintain regular contact: Take the initiative to have regular conversations with your friends. Use various means of communication such as phone calls, text messages, or in-person meetings. Example: Call a friend to check in and have regular discussions.

- **Step 3: Show Interest and Commitment**

Be attentive and receptive: Actively listen and show empathy towards your friends. Demonstrate that you care about their feelings and experiences. Example: When your friend shares a concern or success, show empathy and ask questions to learn more.

- **Step 4: Share Quality Time**

Create opportunities to spend time together: Plan enjoyable activities and share quality moments with your friends. Organize outings, dinners, or common activities that strengthen bonds. Example: Invite your friends for a picnic, a movie night, or an outdoor hike.

- **Step 5: Mutual Support**

Offer emotional support: Be there for your friends when they are going through tough times. Listen without judgment and offer your support and advice if needed. Example: If a friend is going through a stressful period, provide support by actively listening and offering helpful solutions or resources.

- **Step 6: Maintain Authenticity**

Be yourself: Stay authentic in your friendships. Don't be afraid to express your opinions or be vulnerable with your friends. Example: Share your feelings and personal experiences with your friends honestly and be yourself.

By developing these interpersonal relationship skills, you will be able to cultivate and maintain healthy friendships. Take the initiative to initiate relationships, maintain regular communication, show interest and commitment to others, share quality moments, and offer mutual support. These skills will help you create meaningful bonds and strengthen your friendships.

↓ Setting Boundaries :

Knowing how to define and maintain personal boundaries and respecting the boundaries of others in interpersonal relationships.

Practical Sheet: Setting Boundaries

Knowing how to define and maintain personal boundaries is essential for establishing healthy interpersonal relationships. Here is a step-by-step guide to developing this skill:

Step 1: Identify Your Personal Boundaries

- Take the time to reflect on your needs, values, and personal preferences. Identify behaviors, situations, or requests that make you uncomfortable and that you want to limit. **For Example:** You may identify that you need alone time each day to recharge.

Step 2: Be Clear and Specific

- Express your boundaries clearly, specifically, and respectfully. Use affirmative sentences to communicate what you accept and what you do not accept. **For Example:** Say "I prefer to have at least 24 hours' notice before accepting an invitation" rather than "I hate it when people ask me to go out at the last minute."

Step 3: Communicate Your Boundaries Assertively

- Use assertive communication to express your boundaries. Be respectful but firm in your expression, and make sure to maintain an open posture and a calm tone of voice. **For Example:** When someone asks you to do something that goes beyond your boundaries, respond confidently: "I understand that you need help, but I am not able to do it at the moment."

Step 4: Respect the Boundaries of Others

- Recognizing and respecting the boundaries of others is just as important as defining your own. Be attentive to the signals and requests of others, and avoid crossing their personal boundaries. **For Example:** If a friend lets you know that they do not wish to discuss a specific topic, respect their request and do not push them to talk about it.

Step 5: Face the Challenges

- Be prepared to face situations where your boundaries may be questioned or violated. Stand firm in your convictions and do not give in to social pressure or unreasonable demands. **For Example:** If someone tries to convince you to exceed your boundaries, remember the importance of taking care of yourself and maintain your position.

Step 6: Practice Assertive Communication
- Regularly practice communicating your boundaries assertively. The more you practice, the more natural and effective it will become in your interpersonal interactions. **For Example:** Imagine scenarios where you need to express your boundaries and practice corresponding assertive responses.

By developing your boundary-setting skills, you will be able to establish and maintain clear personal boundaries, respect the boundaries of others, and cultivate healthy and balanced interpersonal relationships. Assertive communication is the key to creating respectful relationships where everyone feels heard and respected in their personal boundaries.

↓ Cooperation Skills:
Working effectively in a team, sharing responsibilities, resolving conflicts constructively, and contributing to a common goal.

Practical Sheet: Cooperation Skills
Cooperation skills are essential for working effectively in a team, sharing responsibilities, resolving conflicts constructively, and contributing to a common goal. Here is a step-by-step guide to develop these skills:

- ### Step 1: Establish Clear and Common Goals
Define clear and shared goals with team members. Ensure that everyone understands and is committed to these common goals. **For example:** When working on a team project, set specific goals to achieve and ensure that all team members understand and accept them.

- **Step 2: Sharing Responsibilities**

Distribute responsibilities evenly among team members. Identify each person's strengths and skills to maximize each member's contribution. **For example:** In a project team, assign specific tasks to each member based on their skills and interests. Ensure that each member clearly understands their responsibilities.

- **Step 3: Open and Transparent Communication**

Promote open and transparent communication within the team. Encourage the exchange of ideas, active listening, and respect for everyone's opinions. **For example:** During team meetings, encourage all members to share their ideas and express their concerns. Foster an environment where everyone feels comfortable communicating freely.

- **Step 4: Constructive Conflict Resolution**

In case of conflicts, adopt a constructive resolution approach. Listen to different perspectives, seek mutually acceptable solutions, and prioritize compromise. **For example:** If disagreements arise within the team, organize a discussion to allow each member to express their viewpoint. Encourage the search for solutions that take into account the interests of all members.

- **Step 5: Collaboration and Mutual Support**

Promote collaboration and mutual support among team members. Encourage the sharing of knowledge, experiences, and ideas to achieve common goals. **For example:** Encourage team members to assist each other, share their knowledge, and offer support when a member faces difficulties.

- **Step 6: Evaluation and Continuous Learning**

Conduct regular assessments to identify the strengths and areas for improvement of the team. Use these evaluations to learn and collectively improve. **For example:** After completing a project, organize a team meeting to assess the process, identify successes and challenges, and draw lessons for future projects.

By developing your cooperation skills, you will be able to work effectively as a team, share responsibilities, resolve conflicts constructively, and contribute to a common goal. Cooperation fosters improved productivity, smoother communication, and increased satisfaction within the team.

5. **Social Stress Management Skills:**

⊥ **Social Anxiety Management:**

Develop relaxation, self-soothing, and breathing techniques to manage anxiety in social situations.

Practical Sheet: Social Anxiety Management

Managing social anxiety involves developing relaxation, self-soothing, and breathing techniques to cope with anxiety in social situations. Here is a step-by-step guide to develop these skills:

- **Step 1: Understanding Social Anxiety**

Learn to recognize the signs and symptoms of social anxiety. Understand the negative thoughts and beliefs that can contribute to your anxiety. **For example:** Be aware of physical signs such as a racing heart, sweaty hands, or self-deprecating negative thoughts that occur in social situations.

- **Step 2: Relaxation Techniques**

Learn relaxation techniques to reduce anxiety. This may include methods such as deep breathing, meditation, yoga, or progressive muscle relaxation. **For example:** Practice deep breathing by slowly inhaling through the nose for 4 seconds, holding the breath for 4 seconds, and then exhaling slowly through the mouth for 4 seconds. Repeat several times to relax.

- **Step 3: Self-Soothing**

Develop self-soothing strategies to manage anxiety in social situations. Use positive thoughts, affirmations, and reminders of your own worth and skills. **For example:** When you feel anxious in a social situation, tell yourself positive affirmations such as "I am capable of feeling comfortable and interacting with others" or "I am a kind person worthy of appreciation."

- **Step 4: Gradual Exposure**

Practice gradual exposure to social situations that trigger your anxiety. Start with less stressful situations and gradually progress to more challenging ones. **For example:** Begin by exposing yourself to small social interactions, such as saying hello to a neighbor, then progress to more complex situations, such as participating in a group meeting.

- **Step 5: Social Support**

Seek the support of caring individuals in your circle. Share your feelings and concerns with friends or family members who can provide you with support and encouragement. **For example:** Talk to a trusted friend about your social anxiety difficulties. Ask for their support and consider practicing social situations with them to build confidence.

- **Step 6: Practice and Persistence**

Regularly practice social anxiety management techniques and persevere in your efforts to overcome anxiety. Accept that progress may be gradual and that every step forward counts. **For example:** Commit to practicing relaxation and self-soothing techniques every day, and face social situations with determination and persistence.

By developing your social anxiety management skills, you will be better equipped to handle social situations, reduce your anxiety, and feel more comfortable in interactions with others. Be patient, practice regularly, and don't hesitate to seek additional support if needed, such as cognitive-behavioral therapy, to assist you in your journey of managing social anxiety.

⁙ Social Pressure Management:

Managing peer pressure, social expectations, and assessment situations to maintain a level of confidence and calmness in social interactions.

Practical Sheet: Social Pressure Management

Social pressure management involves dealing with social expectations, peer pressure, and evaluation situations while maintaining a level of confidence and calmness in social interactions. Here is a step-by-step guide to develop these skills:

Step 1: Awareness of Social Pressure

- Become aware of social pressure and the expectations that can influence your behavior and emotions. Identify situations or moments where you feel the most pressure. **For example:** Identify situations such as public presentations, job interviews, or important social events where you feel high social pressure.

Step 2: Challenge Unrealistic Expectations
- Challenge unrealistic expectations you may have of yourself or those imposed by others. Recognize that you cannot please everyone and that it is normal to have imperfections. **For example:** Instead of aiming for perfection, accept that you are doing your best and that making mistakes is a normal part of learning and growth.

Step 3: Identify Your Values and Priorities
- Identify your personal values and priorities. Determine what is truly important to you in order to make decisions that align with your values rather than conforming to the expectations of others. **For example:** Identify your core values such as honesty, authenticity, or work-life balance, and align your actions accordingly.

Step 4: Boost Your Self-Esteem
- Work on your self-esteem by developing a positive perception of yourself. Celebrate your achievements, recognize your strengths, and surround yourself with supportive people. **For example:** Keep a journal where you note your accomplishments, skills, and positive qualities. Practice self-compassion by treating yourself with kindness and understanding.

Step 5: Develop Self-Soothing Strategies
- Develop self-soothing strategies to cope with social pressure. Use relaxation techniques, deep breathing, or visualization to calm your mind and reduce anxiety. **For example:** Before a stressful situation, take a few moments to breathe deeply and imagine yourself feeling calm, confident, and capable of handling the pressure.

<u>**Step 6: Set Healthy Boundaries**</u>

- Establish clear boundaries and adhere to them. Learn to say no when you feel overwhelmed or when others' demands conflict with your values or priorities. **For example:** If you feel overwhelmed by excessive demands, learn to assertively say no while explaining your boundaries and suggesting alternatives if possible.

By developing your skills in managing social pressure, you will be able to maintain a level of confidence and calm in social interactions despite social expectations and peer pressure. Stay true to yourself, respect your boundaries, and use self-soothing strategies to cope with evaluative situations and maintain your emotional well-being.

These social skills can be honed through practical exercises, role-playing, and real interactions with others. By practicing these skills, you can enhance your social ease, strengthen your interpersonal relationships, and feel more comfortable in social situations.

Treatment Planning and Therapeutic Goals

Treatment planning and the establishment of therapeutic goals are key components of cognitive-behavioral therapy. These processes help define the direction of treatment, identify priority areas to work on, and measure progress. Here are the important steps in treatment planning and setting therapeutic goals:

6.1 Setting Therapeutic Goals

Setting clear and specific therapeutic goals is essential for guiding therapeutic work. Therapeutic goals should be formulated in a way that is precise, measurable, achievable, realistic, and time-bound (SMART).

SMART is an acronym used to describe the essential characteristics of therapeutic goals:

- **Specific:** The goal must be clearly defined and specific, focusing on a specific area for improvement.
- **Measurable:** The goal must be measurable to assess progress. Objective criteria should be used to evaluate goal achievement.
- **Achievable:** The goal must be realistic and attainable. It should be aligned with the patient's abilities and resources.
- **Realistic:** The goal must be achievable considering the patient's circumstances and constraints. It should be realistic and in line with the patient's expectations and capabilities.
- **Time-bound:** The goal must have a specific time limit for evaluation. A time period should be established to achieve the goal or to assess progress.

In summary, SMART is a structured approach to setting therapeutic goals that are Specific, Measurable, Achievable, Realistic, and Time-bound. This helps create clear, assessable goals tailored to the patient's situation.

Here is a concrete example to illustrate the establishment of therapeutic goals:

Scenario: A person experiences intense social anxiety and avoids social situations due to fear of judgment and embarrassment.

Therapeutic Objective: Reduce social anxiety and improve participation in social situations.

- **Specific:** Reduce social anxiety specifically related to group situations and social interactions.
- **Measurable:** Evaluate social anxiety using validated assessment scales, such as the Social Anxiety Scale (SAS).
- **Achievable:** Develop strategies for gradual exposure to social situations to progressively and realistically reduce anxiety.
- **Realistic:** Take into account the patient's abilities, resources, and the context in which they operate.
- **Time-bound:** Establish a realistic deadline to observe significant improvements, for example, reducing social anxiety by 50% within three months of starting therapy.

Therapeutic strategies to achieve the goal:

- **Progressive exposure:** Start with less intimidating social situations and gradually increase the level of difficulty by exposing oneself to more complex group situations progressively.
- **Anxiety management techniques:** Learn relaxation, deep breathing, and cognitive restructuring techniques to manage anxiety and associated negative thoughts.
- **Development of social skills:** Enhance communication, assertiveness, and active listening skills to improve social interactions.
- **Utilization of social support:** Encourage seeking support from trusted individuals, such as friends or family members, to strengthen the social network and enhance the feeling of security in social situations.

Setting therapeutic goals helps guide the therapeutic work in a specific manner and measure the progress made. It is important to regularly reassess the goals to adjust them based on the changing needs of the patient and the outcomes achieved.

6.2 Therapy Session Planning

Once the objectives are established, therapy session planning comes into play. The therapist and the patient determine the frequency and duration of the sessions, as well as the specific techniques and interventions that will be used.

Therapy session planning takes into account the patient's needs and preferences, as well as the nature of the issues to be addressed. It may involve a combination of cognitive and behavioral techniques tailored to the specific therapeutic goals.

In the case of self-therapy:

In the case of self-therapy, therapy session planning relies on the individual themselves. It is essential to create a structure and framework to support self-therapy and maximize its benefits. Here are some important elements to consider when planning self-therapy sessions:

1) **Frequency of Sessions:** Determine how often you would like to engage in self-therapy sessions. This can vary depending on your needs and availability. You might opt for regular sessions, for example, You decide to engage in self-therapy sessions once a week, every Sunday afternoon, for a duration of 30 minutes. You block this time in your schedule to ensure that you regularly dedicate time to your emotional well-being.

2) **Session Duration:** Set an appropriate duration for your self-therapy sessions. This can vary depending on your preference and your ability to engage in a practice of reflection and introspection. For example, You establish a duration of 20 minutes for your self-therapy sessions. This allows you to fully concentrate during this period without feeling overwhelmed by a long session. You choose the evening before bedtime to relax and reflect.

3) **Session Structuring:** Develop a structure for your self-therapy sessions to maximize their effectiveness. This can include elements such as reflecting on past experiences, identifying negative automatic thoughts, evaluating these thoughts, and practicing specific techniques such as cognitive restructuring or relaxation. For example, You structure your self-therapy sessions into three parts: (1) Reflection on past experiences and the emotions felt, (2) Identification of negative automatic thoughts and recording them in your thought journal, and (3) Practice of cognitive restructuring by replacing negative thoughts with more adaptive ones.

4) **Use of Tools and Resources:** Identify the tools and resources that can support you in your self-therapy. This can include books, thought journals, online therapy apps, audio recordings of meditation or relaxation, and other resources that can enhance your self-therapy experience.

5) **Monitoring and Evaluation:** Establish a monitoring and evaluation process to measure your progress and adjust your self-therapy practice as needed. This may involve keeping a journal of your sessions, noting any changes or challenges encountered, and reflecting on the results achieved to make informed decisions for the future.

Here is a simple and clear example of a CBT-based self-therapy session to address a stress management issue:

Step 1: Preparation

✓ Find a quiet and comfortable place where you can relax without being disturbed.

✓ Allocate approximately 30 minutes for this self-therapy session.

✓ Make sure you have a journal or notebook to take notes.

Step 2: Relaxation

✓ Start with a relaxation technique to unwind. This can be deep breathing, guided meditation, or a muscle relaxation exercise.

✓ Take a few minutes to center yourself and focus on your breathing.

Step 3: Problem Identification

✓ Identify the stress management problem you want to address in this session. For example, it could be your excessive stress reaction at work.

Step 4: Exploring Automatic Thoughts

✓ Reflect on the automatic thoughts that arise when you are faced with stressful situations at work. Note these thoughts in your journal.
✓ Identify negative or irrational thoughts that contribute to your excessive stress reaction. For example, "I must be perfect, or I am a total failure."

Step 5: Evaluation of Automatic Thoughts

✓ Realistically evaluate the automatic thoughts you have identified. Look for evidence for and against these thoughts.
✓ Challenge cognitive distortions or errors in reasoning present in these thoughts. For example, ask yourself if this demand for perfection is realistic and if it truly contributes to your well-being.

Step 6: Cognitive Restructuring

✓ Replace negative automatic thoughts with more adaptive and realistic thoughts. For example, replace "I must be perfect, or I'm a complete failure" with "I'm doing my best and learning from my mistakes, which is normal and human."
✓ Practice these new thoughts by repeating them aloud or writing them in your journal.

Step 7: Action Plan

✓ Develop a concrete action plan to manage your stress reaction at work. Identify specific strategies such as taking regular breaks, practicing relaxation techniques during stressful moments, or seeking support from colleagues or a therapist.

✓ Set measurable and achievable goals for implementing these strategies into your daily life.

Step 8: Conclusion

✓ Take a moment to recap what you have learned during this self-therapy session.
✓ Record your final reflections and what you intend to put into practice from now on.
Please remember that this example is general, and self-therapy can vary depending on specific issues and individual preferences. It is recommended to consult a mental health professional for additional support and a more precise adaptation to your personal situation.

Self-therapy requires personal discipline and a commitment to your emotional and mental well-being. By planning your self-therapy sessions, structuring your practices, and utilizing available resources, you can create an environment conducive to your personal development and healing.

6.3 Monitoring and Progress Evaluation

Monitoring and progress evaluation are essential to assess the effectiveness of treatment and make necessary adjustments. The therapist and the patient regularly assess the progress made compared to the therapeutic goals set. Various tools can be used to measure progress, such as questionnaires, self-observations, or interviews. These assessments help identify improvements and potential obstacles, and adjust the treatment plan accordingly.

Here is an example of a commonly used questionnaire in cognitive-behavioral therapy to assess symptoms of depression: The Beck Depression Inventory (BDI). Each question is accompanied by a brief explanation of its purpose, and at the end, I will provide an explanation of the meaning of the final score.

Questionnaire: Beck Depression Inventory (BDI)

1. **Sadness: How often do you feel sad or depressed?**
- This question assesses the frequency of feelings of sadness or depression.

2. **Pessimism: How often do you think that nothing will ever get better?**
- This question assesses the level of pessimism and hope for the future.

3. **Feeling of self-devaluation: How often do you feel devalued or worthless?**
- This question assesses self-esteem and self-depreciation.

4. **Guilt: How often do you feel guilty or responsible for things that are not your fault?**
- This question assesses the tendency to feel excessively or inappropriately guilty.

5. **Crying: How often do you cry for no apparent reason?**
– This question assesses the frequency of crying without apparent reason.

6. **Loss of satisfaction: How often do you feel dissatisfied or unable to enjoy things you used to love?**
- This question assesses the loss of pleasure or interest in previously enjoyed activities.

7. **Indecision: How often do you have trouble making decisions?**
- This question assesses difficulties in making decisions.

8. **Loss of Energy: How often do you feel tired or lack energy?**
- This question assesses energy levels and general fatigue.

9. **Appetite Changes: How often have you noticed changes in your appetite (increase or decrease)?**
- This question assesses changes in appetite, such as weight loss or gain.

10. Suicidal Thoughts: How often have you had thoughts of harming yourself or wanting to die?
- This question assesses the presence of suicidal thoughts.

The final IDB score is obtained by assigning points to each response, according to a predefined scale. The total score is used to assess the severity of depressive symptoms. For example, a higher score indicates more severe depression, while a lower score indicates less severe depression. This score can be used to monitor the evolution of symptoms over time and evaluate the effectiveness of treatment. A decrease in the score would indicate an improvement in depressive symptoms.

Regular monitoring and evaluation ensures that treatment is effective, that modifications can be made if necessary, and that patient motivation is maintained throughout the therapeutic process.

Treatment planning and goal setting provide structure and direction to the therapeutic process. They enable us to focus on the specific problems to be addressed, evaluate progress and promote concrete, meaningful results. Working in collaboration with the therapist, the patient can actively engage in his or her own journey towards wellness.

Relapse Management and Prevention

Relapse management and prevention are important aspects of cognitive-behavioral therapy. Relapses can occur after a period of progress, and it is essential to develop strategies to identify and prevent them. Here are some key elements for relapse management and prevention:

7.1 Identifying Signs of Relapse

It is crucial to learn to recognize the early signs of relapse. These signs may vary from person to person but can include increased anxiety or depression, a return of automatic negative thoughts, social withdrawal, decreased motivation, or an increase in problematic behaviors.

Here is a list of potential signs of relapse, along with a brief explanation for each sign:

1. **Increased Anxiety:** A general increase in anxiety may manifest as excessive worry, catastrophic thoughts, or a constant sense of apprehension. **For example:** You begin to experience heightened anxiety in social situations, avoiding interactions with others out of fear of judgment or humiliation.

2. **Increased Depression:** Increased depression can be characterized by feelings of sadness, hopelessness, fatigue, and a loss of interest in once-enjoyed activities. **For example:** You constantly feel sad, struggle to find pleasure in activities you used to enjoy, and your motivation is significantly reduced.

3. **Automatic Negative Thoughts:** Automatic negative thoughts may return more frequently and intensely. This can include thoughts of self-deprecation, pessimism, or despair. **For example:** You constantly criticize yourself, doubting your abilities and seeing yourself as a failure, even when evidence suggests otherwise.

4. **Social Withdrawal:** You may tend to isolate yourself more, avoid social interactions, or feel uncomfortable in the presence of others. **For example:** You begin to cancel plans with friends or avoid social outings, preferring to stay alone at home.

5. **Decreased Motivation:** Your level of motivation may decrease, making it more challenging to accomplish daily tasks or engage in activities that are important to you. **For example:** You struggle to motivate yourself to complete work responsibilities or engage in leisure activities you once enjoyed.

6. **Increased Problematic Behaviors:** You may notice an increase in problematic behaviors, such as avoidance behaviors, impulsive behaviors, or the use of maladaptive defense mechanisms. **For example:** You start using defense mechanisms like projection, consistently attributing problems to others without taking responsibility for your actions.

It is important to note that these signs can vary from person to person. It is recommended to work collaboratively with a mental health professional to identify your specific relapse signs and develop prevention strategies tailored to your personal situation. This may include keeping a tracking journal to note changes in mood, recurring negative thought patterns, or undesirable behaviors. Once relapse signs are identified, prevention strategies can be implemented.

7.2 Relapse Prevention Techniques

Relapse prevention techniques aim to anticipate and avoid potential relapses. Here are some commonly used strategies:

- **Maintenance of Acquired Skills:**

Once effective skills and strategies have been developed during therapy, it is important to continue practicing and reinforcing them regularly. This may include the ongoing use of cognitive techniques, behavioral techniques, and stress management skills learned during therapy.

How?

To maintain the skills acquired during therapy, here are some suggestions:

1) **Regular Practice:** Continue to implement the skills and strategies learned during therapy in your daily life. Repeat exercises, relaxation techniques, cognitive restructuring, and problem-solving skills regularly to reinforce these abilities.

2) **Self-Observation:** Continue to observe your thoughts, emotions, and behaviors using the self-observation skills developed during therapy. Be aware of your thought patterns, emotional reactions, and behaviors to adjust them if necessary.

3) **Journaling:** Keep a journal to document your thoughts, emotions, and behaviors. This can help you spot recurring patterns, identify situations that trigger problematic reactions, and assess your progress over time.

4) **Positive Reinforcement:** Congratulate and reward yourself when you successfully use the skills acquired during therapy. Celebrate your successes and acknowledge the progress you've made, even the smallest ones.

5) **Regular Review of Techniques:** Regularly revisit the exercises and techniques learned during therapy to ensure you keep them fresh in your memory. This may include reviewing your notes, going over your action plan, or practicing relaxation exercises again.

6) **Social Support:** Surround yourself with people who support your growth and well-being. Share your experiences, successes, and challenges with friends, loved ones, or support groups that can encourage you and provide emotional support.

7) **Regular Follow-Up:** If possible, consider maintaining regular follow-ups with your therapist or attending periodic maintenance sessions to discuss your progress, address new challenges, and receive additional guidance.

By regularly practicing the skills learned during therapy, you strengthen your ability to cope with challenges and maintain your emotional well-being. Remember that self-help can be complemented by the professional support of a therapist if needed.

- **Planning Adaptation Strategies:**

The patient and the therapist can work together to develop a specific action plan in case of signs of relapse. This may include identifying alternative coping strategies, seeking social support, using relaxation techniques, or engaging in enjoyable activities to counter early relapse symptoms.

How?

Here is an example of steps for planning adaptation strategies in case of relapse signs:

1) **Identification of relapse signs:** Work with your therapist to identify the specific signs of relapse that are unique to your situation. This may include mood changes, recurrent negative thoughts, or problematic behaviors.

2) **List of coping strategies:** Together, create a list of coping strategies that can help you deal with signs of relapse. This may include relaxation techniques, mindfulness activities, the use of cognitive techniques, engaging in enjoyable activities, or seeking social support.

3) **Development of an action plan:** Based on the list of coping strategies, create a detailed action plan for each identified sign of relapse. For example, if you notice an increase in anxiety, your action plan could include practicing deep breathing techniques or engaging in relaxing activities.

4) **Putting into practice:** Regularly practice the identified coping strategies, even when you do not feel any signs of relapse. This will help you strengthen these skills and have them at your disposal when you need them.

5) **Regular review:** Regularly review your action plan with your therapist to ensure it remains suitable for your current situation. You can make adjustments or add new strategies based on your changing needs.

6) **Use of visual aids:** To make your action plan more concrete, you can create a mind map, a chart, or a visual list with specific coping strategies for each sign of relapse. This can help you easily remember the steps to take when you encounter difficulties.

7) **Regular practice:** Practice coping strategies regularly, even when you are feeling well. This will help you strengthen these skills and make them more accessible when you need them.

Planning coping strategies helps you be better prepared to deal with signs of relapse and to act quickly to reduce their impact. Working in collaboration with your therapist is essential for developing a personalized action plan tailored to your specific needs.

- **Strengthening Support Resources:**

It's important to identify and strengthen available support resources, whether it's family, friends, support groups, or healthcare professionals. Maintaining good communication with these individuals can be valuable in case you need additional support.

Here are some steps to strengthen your support resources:

1) **Identification of Support Resources:** Identify the individuals or groups that can be a source of support in your life. This may include family members, close friends, trusted colleagues, online support groups, or mental health professionals.

2) **Open Communication:** Maintain open and honest communication with your support resources. Share your needs, challenges, and progress with them. Be prepared to ask for help when you need it and be receptive to their support.

3) **Regularly Connect:** Schedule regular times to interact with your support resources. This can include in-person meetings, phone calls, messaging, or participating in group meetings. Maintaining a regular connection strengthens your support network.

4) **Express Your Needs:** Be clear about your needs and expectations from your support resources. Communicate openly about what would help you the most during difficult times. This can be a simple need for listening, advice, or positive distractions.

5) **Offer Support in Return:** Support is a two-way relationship. Be ready to support your support resources when possible. Actively listen, provide encouragement, and be there for them when they need it.

6) **Explore New Resources:** If you feel that your current support resources are limited, seek out new opportunities to expand your

support network. This can include joining community groups, searching for online support groups, or consulting with mental health professionals for additional guidance.

7) **Be Grateful:** Show your gratitude to your support resources. Express your appreciation for their presence and support in your life. This strengthens the bonds and encourages an ongoing relationship of mutual support.

By strengthening your support resources, you create a strong network that can help you face challenges and maintain your emotional well-being. Remember that the professional support of a therapist can also be a valuable resource to include in your support plan.

- **Self-Management and Regular Monitoring:**

Encourage the patient to become an active participant in their own mental health by practicing self-management and taking proactive care of themselves. This can include continuing self-care techniques, regular physical exercise, a balanced diet, appropriate stress management, and seeking professional support if needed.

Here are some suggestions for self-management and regular monitoring of your mental well-being:

✓ **Practice Self-Care Techniques:** Identify self-care techniques that work best for you, such as meditation, deep breathing, yoga, journal writing, creative activities, inspirational reading, or any other activities that bring you comfort and relaxation. Incorporate these practices into your daily routine to take care of yourself.

✓ **Regular Physical Exercise:** Physical activity has a positive impact on your mental well-being. Find a form of exercise you enjoy, whether it's walking, running, cycling, dancing, or a sport. Try to engage in regular physical activity to boost your energy, reduce stress, and improve your mood.

✓ **Balanced Diet:** Ensure you maintain a balanced and nutritious diet. Consume foods rich in nutrients, vitamins, and minerals. Avoid processed foods and added sugars as much as possible, as they can impact your energy and mood.

- ✓ **Stress Management:** Learn stress management techniques such as relaxation, meditation, or time management. Identify stressful situations in your life and find healthy and effective ways to manage them. Take regular breaks and engage in activities that relax you and allow you to recharge.
- ✓ **Regular Monitoring:** Maintain regular monitoring of your mental well-being. Reflect on your mood, emotions, and stress level. If you notice signs of deteriorating mental health, take steps to seek additional support, whether by turning to a mental health professional or utilizing available support resources.
- ✓ **Prioritize Yourself:** Take time to care for yourself and your needs. Allow yourself moments of relaxation, activities you enjoy, and opportunities to recharge. Learn to say no when you need rest or time for yourself.

Self-management and regular monitoring allow you to take an active role in your mental well-being. By adopting self-care practices, maintaining regular physical activity, eating a balanced diet, managing stress, and staying attentive to your mental health, you create the conditions for your growth and ongoing well-being.

By implementing these relapse prevention strategies, the patient is better prepared to face potential difficulties and maintain the progress made during therapy. This promotes greater resilience and a better ability to prevent relapses and sustain lasting mental well-being.

It is important to note that relapse management and prevention are ongoing processes. Patients may experience ups and downs throughout their journey, and facing challenges is normal. Cognitive-behavioral therapy provides the tools and strategies necessary to deal with these situations and continue moving towards optimal mental well-being.

Specific Applications of Cognitive-Behavioral Therapy

Cognitive-behavioral therapy is a versatile approach that can be used to treat a variety of psychological issues. Here are some specific applications of CBT:

8.1 Anxiety and Panic Disorders:

CBT is effective in treating anxiety and panic disorders. It uses techniques such as graduated exposure, response prevention, cognitive restructuring, and anxiety management skills training to help individuals overcome their fears and reduce excessive anxiety.

Fact Sheet: Specific Applications of CBT in Anxiety and Panic Disorders

Cognitive-behavioral therapy (CBT) is an effective approach for treating anxiety and panic disorders. Here is a step-by-step guide for applying CBT in these areas:

Step 1: Initial Assessment

- Conduct a thorough initial assessment to understand the patient's symptoms, stress factors, and history. Use standardized assessment tools to evaluate anxiety and panic disorders. **For example:** Use self-assessment questionnaires such as the Beck Anxiety Inventory (BAI) or the Panic and Agoraphobia Scale (PAS) to assess the severity of symptoms.

Step 2: Psychoeducation

- Provide psychoeducation to the patient about anxiety and panic disorders. Explain the underlying mechanisms, irrational thoughts, and physical reactions associated with anxiety. **For example:** Explain how catastrophic thoughts can trigger panic attacks and how intense physical sensations can be attributed to normal bodily reactions to anxiety.

Step 3: Identification of Automatic Thoughts

- Help the patient identify and recognize negative automatic thoughts that contribute to anxiety and panic attacks. Encourage them to note these thoughts in a journal. **For example:** Encourage the patient to record negative thoughts that arise during a panic attack, such as "I'm going to faint" or "I'm going to lose control."

Step 4: Evaluation of Automatic Thoughts

- Evaluate the validity and reality of automatic thoughts using questioning techniques. Help the patient examine the evidence for and against these negative thoughts. **For example:** Ask the patient to consider the evidence for and against their automatic thought, such as asking "What is the evidence that I will faint?" or "What is the evidence that this has happened in the past?".

Step 5: Cognitive Restructuring

- Assist the patient in restructuring their negative automatic thoughts by identifying more realistic and positive alternative thoughts. Train them to replace negative thoughts with these alternative thoughts. **For example:** Encourage the patient to replace the thought "I will faint" with alternative thoughts like "It is unlikely that I will faint because it has never happened before".

Step 6: Exposure and Response Prevention

- Use exposure techniques to help the patient gradually confront their fears and anxiety-provoking situations. Teach them strategies to manage physical anxiety responses. **For example:** Gradually expose the patient to anxiety-inducing situations, such as going to public places, while teaching them to use relaxation, breathing, and muscle relaxation techniques to reduce anxiety.

Step 7: Learning Coping Skills

- Teach the patient coping skills such as stress management, problem-solving, and assertive communication to deal with stressful situations and prevent relapses. **For example:** Teach the patient stress management techniques, such as self-care planning and regular practice of relaxation activities, to help them manage stressful situations that could trigger anxiety.

<u>**Step 8: Monitoring and Progress Evaluation**</u>
- Conduct regular assessments to measure the patient's progress in reducing anxiety and panic symptoms. Adjust the treatment plan if necessary and encourage the patient to maintain the gains. **For example:** Use periodic assessment questionnaires such as the Hamilton Anxiety Rating Scale (HAM-A) to assess changes in anxiety levels and adjust interventions accordingly.

By following these steps, you will be able to apply CBT specifically for anxiety and panic disorders. Identifying automatic thoughts, cognitive restructuring, graduated exposure, and learning adaptation skills will play a key role in reducing symptoms and improving the patient's well-being.

8.2 Depression:

CBT is widely used to treat depression. It focuses on cognitive restructuring to identify and modify negative thought patterns, as well as behavioral activation to encourage engagement in pleasurable and rewarding activities. CBT helps individuals acquire skills to manage depression symptoms and develop positive coping strategies.

Practical Sheet: Specific Applications of CBT in Depression

Cognitive-Behavioral Therapy (CBT) is an effective approach for treating depression. It focuses on modifying negative thought patterns, promoting adaptive behaviors, and strengthening the patient's resources. Here is a detailed step-by-step guide for applying CBT in the treatment of depression:

<u>**Step 1: Initial Assessment**</u>
- Conduct a comprehensive initial assessment of the patient's depression. Identify specific symptoms, personal and family history, stressors, and available resources. **For example:** Use self-assessment questionnaires such as the Beck Depression Inventory (BDI) to assess the severity of depressive symptoms.

<u>**Step 2: Case Formulation**</u>
- Develop a case formulation that identifies factors contributing to the patient's depression, such as negative thought patterns, triggering events, and avoidance behaviors.

Example: Identify negative automatic thought patterns, such as self-deprecation and cognitive distortion, that maintain the patient's depression.

Step 3: Setting Therapeutic Goals

- Collaboratively with the patient, define specific, measurable, achievable, relevant, and time-bound (SMART) therapeutic goals. Goals should focus on reducing depressive symptoms, improving functioning, and preventing relapses. **For example:** A SMART therapeutic goal could be for the patient to reduce depressive symptoms measured by the BDI by 50% within 3 months.

Step 4: Cognitive Techniques

- Teach the patient cognitive techniques to identify, assess, and restructure negative thoughts. Help them challenge cognitive distortions and develop more realistic and positive thoughts. **For example:** Use the "thought column" exercise to assist the patient in identifying and restructuring automatic negative thoughts.

Step 5: Behavioral Techniques

- Introduce behavioral techniques to increase activity and engagement in enjoyable activities. Encourage the patient to identify and break the cycles of inactivity and social withdrawal. **For example:** Use behavioral activation to help the patient plan and engage in pleasurable activities, even if they do not immediately feel pleasure.

Step 6: Problem-Solving Skills Training

- Teach the patient problem-solving skills to help cope with daily challenges and find alternative solutions. Encourage the exploration of different options and the evaluation of potential consequences. **For example:** Guide the patient through a structured problem-solving procedure, helping them identify problems, generate solutions, and choose the best option.

Step 7: Monitoring and Progress Evaluation

- Conduct regular assessments to evaluate the patient's progress towards therapeutic goals. Readjust interventions as needed and encourage the patient to maintain gains and practice learned skills. **For example:** Use regular follow-up questionnaires to assess the patient's depressive symptoms and monitor changes over time.

Cognitive-Behavioral Therapy (CBT) in the treatment of depression combines cognitive, behavioral, and skills training techniques to help patients change their negative thought patterns, increase engagement in positive activities, and develop problem-solving skills. By following this step-by-step approach, therapists can effectively guide their patients in their journey toward reducing depressive symptoms and improving emotional well-being.

8.3 Eating Disorders:

CBT is often used in the treatment of eating disorders such as anorexia, bulimia, and binge-eating disorder. It focuses on cognitive restructuring of dysfunctional thoughts related to body image, food, and emotion management. CBT also helps develop behavioral strategies to regulate eating behaviors.

Practical Sheet: Specific Applications of CBT in Eating Disorders

Cognitive-Behavioral Therapy (CBT) offers effective approaches for treating eating disorders such as anorexia, bulimia, and binge-eating disorder. Here is a detailed step-by-step guide for applying CBT in eating disorders:

Step 1: Initial Assessment

- Implement the treatment plan by working collaboratively with the patient. Use CBT techniques to help the patient develop skills in intuitive eating, manage difficult emotions, and improve self-esteem. **For example:** During therapy sessions, guide the patient through cognitive restructuring exercises to identify cognitive distortions related to eating and body image, and use gradual exposure techniques to reduce food avoidance behaviors.

Step 2: Case Formulation

- Develop a case formulation that integrates the information gathered during the initial assessment. Identify the factors maintaining the eating disorders, such as unrealistic beliefs about weight and appearance, dysfunctional thought patterns, and restrictive or compensatory behaviors. **For example:** Identify how perfectionistic beliefs and restrictive behaviors have contributed to the patient's anorexia, maintaining a cycle of excessive weight loss and strict food control.

Step 3: Setting Therapeutic Goals

- Establish specific therapeutic goals in collaboration with the patient, focusing on problematic eating behaviors, emotional regulation, and improvement of self-esteem. Goals should be achievable and measurable. For example: A therapeutic goal could be for the patient to reach a healthy weight by adopting balanced eating habits and modifying negative thoughts related to physical appearance.

Step 4: Intervention Planning

· Develop a detailed intervention plan using techniques and strategies specific to CBT for eating disorders. Identify interventions such as psychoeducation, cognitive restructuring, emotion management, meal planning, and gradual exposure to feared foods. **For example:** Plan therapy sessions focused on identifying dysfunctional thoughts related to eating, cognitive restructuring to change unrealistic beliefs, and gradual exposure to feared foods to reduce avoidance behaviors.

Step 5: Treatment Implementation

Implement the treatment plan by working collaboratively with the patient. Use CBT techniques to help the patient develop skills in intuitive eating, manage difficult emotions, and improve self-esteem. **For example:** During therapy sessions, guide the patient through cognitive restructuring exercises to identify cognitive distortions related to eating and body image, and use gradual exposure techniques to reduce food avoidance behaviors.

Step 6: Monitoring and Progress Evaluation

- Conduct regular assessments to measure the patient's progress towards therapeutic goals. Adjust interventions as necessary and encourage the patient to maintain the gains and continue working on difficulties. **For example:** Use periodic self-assessment questionnaires to evaluate the patient's eating behaviors, emotions related to eating, and self-esteem, and adjust interventions accordingly.

By following these steps, you will be able to effectively implement CBT in the treatment of eating disorders. Initial assessment, case formulation, establishment of therapeutic goals, intervention planning, treatment implementation, and progress monitoring will allow you to work in a targeted and systematic way to help the patient develop healthy eating habits, improve self-esteem, and overcome difficulties associated with eating disorders.

8.4 Obsessive-Compulsive Disorders (OCD):

CBT is considered one of the most effective approaches for treating OCD. It uses exposure and response prevention techniques to help individuals confront their obsessions and reduce compulsive behaviors. CBT helps modify thought patterns related to obsessions and develop strategies to manage OCD symptoms.

Practical Sheet: Specific Applications of CBT in Obsessive-Compulsive Disorders (OCD)

Obsessive-Compulsive Disorders (OCD) are anxiety disorders characterized by the presence of recurrent obsessions and repetitive compulsions. Cognitive-behavioral therapy (CBT) is widely recognized as an effective approach in treating OCD. Here is a step-by-step guide for the application of CBT in the treatment of OCD:

Step 1: Initial Assessment

- Conduct a comprehensive assessment of OCD symptoms, including obsessions, compulsions, triggering factors, and functional impact on the patient's daily life. Use standardized assessment tools to evaluate the severity of symptoms. **For example:** Use the Hospital Anxiety and Depression Scale (HADS) to measure the severity of anxiety and depression in a patient with OCD.

Step 2: Psychoeducation

- Provide educational information to the patient about OCD, its causes, mechanisms, and available treatment options. Help the patient understand that OCD is an anxiety disorder and that obsessions are intrusive thoughts that do not reflect reality. **For example:** Explain to the patient that obsessions are involuntary thoughts, and compulsions are repetitive behaviors aimed at reducing anxiety but can become counterproductive in the long term.

Step 3: Exposure Hierarchy

- Assist the patient in establishing a hierarchy of graduated exposures, starting with situations that cause moderate anxiety and progressing to the most feared situations. Identify specific obsessions and compulsive behaviors associated with each situation. **For example:** For a patient with a contamination obsession, the hierarchy may begin with touching lightly dirty objects and progress to more anxiety-provoking situations, such as touching potentially contaminated objects.

Step 4: Exposure and Response Prevention

- Implement exposure sessions by progressively and controlledly exposing the patient to feared situations from the exposure hierarchy. Encourage the patient to resist engaging in compulsions using response prevention strategies. **For example:** In the case of a patient with a contamination obsession, expose them to mildly dirty objects and encourage them to resist the temptation to immediately wash their hands.

Step 5: Cognitive Restructuring

- Work with the patient to identify and challenge unrealistic obsessive thoughts and harmful beliefs associated with OCD. Teach cognitive restructuring techniques to help the patient modify dysfunctional thought patterns. **For example:** Help the patient identify automatic thoughts such as *"If I don't wash my hands, I will get sick"* and replace them with more realistic thoughts like *"It is unlikely that I will get sick from touching this object."*

Step 6: Maintenance and Relapse Prevention

- Ensure that the patient has maintenance strategies to sustain the progress made and prevent relapses. Encourage regular practice of the techniques learned during therapy and provide additional support resources if needed. **For Example:** Recommend that the patient continue regular exposure to anxiety-provoking situations, use self-help strategies such as relaxation, and involve loved ones in ongoing support.

By using these steps in the application of CBT in the treatment of OCD, you will be able to help the patient confront their obsessions and reduce their compulsive behaviors. The combination of graded exposure, response prevention, and cognitive restructuring is crucial in assisting the patient in overcoming OCD symptoms and improving their quality of life.

8.5 Personality Disorders:

CBT can be used to treat personality disorders such as borderline personality disorder, avoidant personality disorder, or dependent personality disorder. It focuses on modifying maladaptive thought patterns and behaviors, as well as developing healthier and more functional coping skills.

Practical Sheet: Specific Applications of CBT in Personality Disorders

Cognitive-behavioral therapy (CBT) can be an effective tool in treating personality disorders. Here is a detailed step-by-step guide for the application of CBT in personality disorders:

Step 1: Initial Assessment

- Conduct a comprehensive initial assessment of the patient, gathering information about their personal history, symptoms, thought patterns, and problematic behaviors related to their personality disorder. **For example:** Identify rigid thought patterns, impulsive behaviors, or specific interpersonal difficulties associated with the patient's personality disorder.

Step 2: Case Formulation

- Develop a case formulation that integrates the information gathered during the initial assessment. Identify factors maintaining the patient's symptoms, such as limiting beliefs, dysfunctional behavioral habits, or triggering events. **For example:** Identify how negative abandonment-related thought patterns have influenced the patient's avoidance behaviors and interpersonal difficulties.

Step 3: Establishing Therapeutic Goals

- Establish clear, specific, and measurable therapeutic goals in collaboration with the patient. The goals should focus on changing thoughts, behaviors, and dysfunctional patterns associated with the personality disorder. **For example:** A therapeutic goal could be for the patient to develop assertiveness skills to improve interpersonal relationships and reduce self-devaluation.

Step 4: Intervention Planning

- Develop a detailed intervention plan using CBT techniques and strategies tailored to personality disorders. Identify specific interventions to implement in order to achieve therapeutic goals. **For example:** Plan therapy sessions focused on techniques such as cognitive restructuring, emotion regulation skills training, mindfulness therapy, and graduated exposure to address the patient's dysfunctional thought patterns.

Step 5: Treatment Implementation

- Implement the treatment plan by working collaboratively with the patient. Use CBT techniques to help the patient develop emotional regulation skills, change limiting thought patterns, and adopt more adaptive behaviors. **For example:** During therapy sessions, guide the patient through cognitive restructuring exercises to challenge automatic negative thoughts associated with their personality disorder.

Step 6: Monitoring and Progress Evaluation

- Conduct regular assessments to evaluate the progress made by the patient towards therapeutic goals. Adjust interventions as necessary and encourage the patient to maintain their achievements and continue working on specific personality disorder-related challenges. **For example:** Use symptom assessment scales and follow-up questionnaires to assess changes in thought patterns, behaviors, and symptoms associated with the personality disorder.

By following these steps, you will be able to systematically plan the treatment of personality disorders and establish appropriate therapeutic goals in CBT. A strong case formulation and detailed intervention plan will guide you in applying specific CBT techniques tailored to the patient's personality disorder.

8.6 Sleep Disorders:

CBT is effective in treating sleep disorders such as insomnia. It utilizes techniques like sleep restriction, relaxation, and cognitive restructuring to improve sleep quality and duration.

Practical Sheet: Specific Applications of CBT in Sleep Disorders

Cognitive-behavioral therapy (CBT) offers effective approaches to treating sleep disorders such as insomnia and sleep apnea. Here is a detailed step-by-step guide for applying CBT in sleep disorders:

Step 1: Initial Assessment

- Conduct a comprehensive assessment of the sleep disorder by gathering information on sleep patterns, sleep habits, stress factors, emotions, and sleep-related behaviors. Use standardized assessment tools if necessary. **For example:** Conduct in-depth clinical interviews and utilize self-assessment questionnaires to evaluate sleep quality, sleep habits, and associated disorders such as anxiety or depression.

Step 2: Case Formulation

- Develop a case formulation that identifies the factors maintaining the sleep disorder, such as anxious thoughts related to sleep, irregular sleep habits, or disruptive environmental factors. **For example:** Identify how sleep-related concerns and irregular sleep habits contribute to the patient's insomnia, triggering a vicious cycle of anxiety and poor sleep quality.

Step 3: Establishment of Therapeutic Objectives

- Establish specific and measurable therapeutic objectives in collaboration with the patient. Objectives may include improving sleep quality, reducing insomnia symptoms, and adopting healthy sleep behaviors. **For example:** A therapeutic objective could be for the patient

86

to achieve six hours of continuous sleep per night and feel rested and energized during the day.

Step 4: CBT Techniques for Sleep Disorders

- Use specific CBT techniques to treat sleep disorders, such as sleep restriction, sleep hygiene, and relaxation.

Example:

✓ Sleep Restriction: Establish a regular sleep routine by limiting time spent in bed only for sleep and avoiding excessive napping.

✓ Sleep Hygiene: Adopt healthy bedtime practices, such as creating a conducive sleep environment, avoiding stimulants and screens before bedtime, and promoting relaxation.

✓ Relaxation Techniques: Learn relaxation techniques, such as deep breathing, meditation, or muscle relaxation, to reduce anxiety and promote restful sleep.

Step 5: Treatment Implementation

- Implement the treatment plan by working collaboratively with the patient. Encourage the practice of learned techniques, keeping a sleep journal, and monitoring progress. **For example:** Encourage the patient to keep a sleep journal to track sleep patterns, levels of fatigue, and factors influencing sleep quality. Use this information to adjust interventions and measure progress.

Step 6: Monitoring and Progress Evaluation

- Conduct regular assessments to evaluate the patient's progress towards therapeutic goals. Adjust interventions as necessary and encourage the patient to maintain healthy sleep habits in the long term.

Example: Conduct regular follow-ups to assess changes in the patient's sleep quality, adoption of new sleep habits, and reduction of insomnia symptoms. Adjust techniques based on the results obtained.

By following these steps, CBT can help individuals suffering from sleep disorders improve their sleep quality, reduce insomnia symptoms, and adopt healthy sleep habits. A comprehensive initial assessment, precise case formulation, and the application of specific CBT techniques enable the development of an individualized and effective treatment plan for sleep disorders.

8.7 Stress Management:

CBT is used to help individuals effectively manage stress. It teaches relaxation techniques, problem-solving skills, cognitive restructuring, and time management to reduce stress reactions and promote optimal mental well-being.

Fact Sheet: Specific Applications of CBT in Stress Management

Cognitive-Behavioral Therapy (CBT) provides effective tools and strategies for managing stress. Here is a detailed step-by-step guide for applying CBT in stress management:

Step 1: Stress Level Assessment

- Start by assessing your current stress level. Identify the situations, thoughts, and emotions contributing to your stress. **For example:** Take note of specific situations where you feel the most stress, such as tight work deadlines or interpersonal conflicts.

Step 2: Identifying Stressful Thoughts

- Identify the negative automatic thoughts contributing to your stress. Become aware of negative and irrational thinking patterns. **For example:** Identify thoughts such as "I can't handle this situation" or "Everything will go wrong."

Step 3: Cognitive Restructuring

- Use the cognitive restructuring technique to modify stressful thoughts. Replace negative thoughts with more realistic and positive ones. **For example:** Replace the thought "I can't handle this situation" with "I can find solutions and effectively manage this situation."

Step 4: Emotion Management

- Learn emotion management techniques to regulate emotional stress. Practice relaxation techniques such as deep breathing or meditation to calm the body and mind. **For example:** Take a few minutes each day to relax and practice deep breathing exercises.

Step 5: Managing Stress-Related Behaviors
- Identify problematic behaviors that can worsen your stress, such as procrastination or avoidance. Develop strategies to change these behaviors and adopt more adaptive reactions. **For example:** Create an action plan to manage stressful tasks by breaking them down into smaller steps and setting realistic deadlines.

Step 6: Time and Activity Management
- Use time management techniques to better organize your activities and reduce time-related sources of stress. **For example:** Use a planner or calendar to schedule your tasks and activities realistically, allowing enough time for breaks and relaxation.

Step 7: Assertive Communication
- Learn to communicate assertively to express your needs and boundaries clearly and respectfully, thereby reducing conflicts and interpersonal stress. **For example:** Practice expressing your needs and boundaries in challenging communication situations, using affirmative phrases and expressing your emotions constructively.

Step 8: Relapse Prevention
- Develop strategies to prevent long-term stress relapses. Identify potential stressors and establish coping mechanisms to proactively address them. **For example:** Identify situations or events that can trigger your stress and develop action plans to preventively manage them.

By following these steps, you will be able to effectively apply cognitive-behavioral therapy in stress management. CBT provides concrete tools to modify stressful thoughts, regulate emotions, adopt adaptive behaviors, and prevent relapses. Feel free to consult a qualified therapist to guide you through this process.

8.8 Addiction and Dependency:

CBT is used in the treatment of addictions and dependencies, such as alcohol addiction, drug addiction, or gambling addiction. It focuses on identifying thought patterns and behaviors associated with addiction, as well as strengthening resistance and craving management skills.

Practical Sheet: Specific Applications of CBT in Addiction and Dependency

Cognitive Behavioral Therapy (CBT) is a widely used clinical approach in the treatment of addiction and dependency. It focuses on identifying dysfunctional thought patterns and behaviors associated with addiction, as well as developing strategies to modify them and promote lasting remission. Here is a step-by-step guide to applying CBT in the treatment of addiction and dependency:

Step 1: Initial Assessment

- Conduct a comprehensive assessment of the dependency and its physical, psychological, and social consequences. Gather information about consumption history, stress factors, triggers, and negative consequences associated with addiction.

Step 2: Education and Awareness

- Provide educational information about addiction and its mechanisms to help the patient understand the biological, psychological, and social aspects of their dependency. Assist them in becoming aware of the thoughts, emotions, and behaviors associated with their addiction.

Step 3: Identification of Triggers and Thought Patterns

- Help the patient identify internal and external triggers that contribute to their addictive consumption. Work on recognizing dysfunctional thought patterns related to addiction, such as thoughts of justification, minimization, or denial.

Step 4: Cognitive Restructuring

- Use cognitive restructuring techniques to help the patient challenge and modify their negative and dysfunctional thought patterns. Encourage exploration of underlying beliefs and the search for contradictory evidence to support more positive and realistic thoughts.

Step 5: Craving and Consumption Behavior Management

- Learn craving and consumption behavior management techniques to help the patient deal with high-risk situations and resist the urge to consume. Use techniques such as relapse prevention, self-monitoring, and the use of healthy coping strategies.

Step 6: Developing Alternative Life Skills

- Help the patient develop alternative and healthy life skills to replace consumption behaviors. Identify positive activities, stress management strategies, and problem-solving techniques to promote a balanced and fulfilling lifestyle.

Step 7: Social Support and Support Networks

- Encourage the patient to engage in support networks, such as peer support groups or recovery programs, to strengthen social support and mutual assistance. Promote effective communication and encourage active participation in these networks.

Step 8: Follow-up and Relapse Prevention

- Schedule regular follow-up sessions to assess the patient's progress, reinforce acquired skills, and prevent relapses. Use relapse prevention techniques such as identifying relapse signs, creating an action plan, and developing strategies for managing high-risk situations.

Step 9: Long-term Supportive Care

- Facilitate access to long-term supportive care to help the patient maintain their progress and cope with post-treatment challenges. Encourage participation in follow-up therapies, support groups, and other relevant community resources.

By applying these CBT steps in the treatment of addiction and dependence, you can help the patient understand and modify the thought and behavior patterns related to their addiction, develop skills for managing cravings and consumption behaviors, strengthen their social support, and prevent relapses. CBT provides a structured and effective approach to support remission and promote a sober and balanced lifestyle.

8.9 Time Management Problems:

CBT can be used to help individuals improve their time management and develop strategies for planning, task prioritization, and distraction management. It can be helpful for people who have difficulty organizing their time and achieving their goals.

Fact Sheet: Time Management Issues in CBT

Cognitive-behavioral therapy (CBT) can be successfully applied to address time management issues. Here is a detailed step-by-step guide on using CBT in time management:

Step 1: Initial Assessment

- Conduct a comprehensive initial assessment to understand the patient's specific time management difficulties. Identify problematic behaviors, limiting beliefs, and barriers that hinder effective time utilization.

Example: Identify if the patient struggles with setting priorities, managing distractions, or organizing their schedule.

Step 2: Therapeutic Goal Setting

- Collaboratively establish clear and specific therapeutic goals with the patient. The goals should be tailored to the identified time management issues and focus on improving time management skills.

Example: A therapeutic goal could be for the patient to be able to create a structured and realistic schedule to effectively manage their responsibilities and activities.

Step 3: Identification of Limiting Thoughts and Beliefs

- Assist the patient in identifying limiting thoughts and beliefs that contribute to poor time management. Explore beliefs such as procrastination, perfectionism, or difficulty in saying no.

Example: Identify if the patient tends to think "I can't start until I'm sure I can do it perfectly" or "I don't want to disappoint others by refusing their requests."

Step 4: Cognitive Restructuring

- Work with the patient to restructure thoughts and limiting beliefs related to time management. Help them adopt more adaptive and realistic thoughts that promote more effective time management.

Example: Replace the belief "I have to do everything perfectly" with "I can do my best in the available time, and that will be enough."

Step 5: Development of Time Management Skills

- Teach the patient practical time management skills to improve their efficiency. This may include planning, task prioritization, handling interruptions, delegation, stress management, and the use of tools such as to-do lists and calendars.

Example: Teach the patient planning techniques, such as creating a daily to-do list and prioritizing tasks based on their importance and urgency.

Step 6: Gradual Exposure and Reinforcement

- Use gradual exposure techniques to help the patient gradually expose themselves to situations that may be challenging in terms of time management. Reinforce positive behaviors related to effective time management.

Example: Encourage the patient to engage in a challenging task by offering positive reinforcements such as enjoyable breaks or rewards after completing the task.

Step 7: Monitoring and Progress Evaluation

- Regularly evaluate the patient's progress towards therapeutic goals. Adjust interventions as needed and encourage the patient to maintain new time management skills.

Example: Use self-assessment tools such as time tracking journals or time management rating scales to assess the patient's progress.

By following these steps, you will be able to use CBT in a structured manner to help individuals improve their time management. The combination of thorough assessment, identification of limiting thoughts, cognitive restructuring, practical skill development, and gradual implementation will enable the patient to better manage their time and achieve their goals more effectively.

8.10 Specific Phobias:

Cognitive-behavioral therapy (CBT) is effective in treating specific phobias, such as the fear of heights, animals, or enclosed spaces. It uses gradual exposure techniques to help individuals confront their fears progressively and reduce associated anxiety.

Practical Sheet: Specific Applications of CBT in Specific Phobias

Specific phobias are intense and irrational fears related to specific objects, situations, or activities. Cognitive-behavioral therapy (CBT) offers effective techniques for treating specific phobias. Here is a step-by-step guide to applying CBT in the treatment of specific phobias:

Step 1: Initial Assessment
- Conduct a detailed initial assessment of the patient's specific phobia, gathering information about the nature of the phobia, triggering situations, and its impact on the patient's daily life.

Example: Identify the patient's specific phobia, such as a fear of spiders, by describing the situations where the fear is triggered and the consequences of the phobia on the patient's life.

Step 2: Education on the Phobia
- Provide the patient with educational information about the specific phobia, explaining the mechanisms of fear, physiological reactions, and irrational thoughts associated with the phobia.

Example: Explain to the patient that an intense fear of spiders is a natural reaction but can be exaggerated and irrational in the case of a specific phobia.

Step 3: Cognitive Restructuring
- Assist the patient in identifying and challenging irrational thoughts associated with the specific phobia. Teach cognitive restructuring

techniques to replace negative thoughts with more realistic and positive ones.

Example: Encourage the patient to identify negative thoughts such as "All spiders are dangerous" and replace them with more realistic thoughts like "Most spiders are harmless and won't harm me."

Step 4: Progressive Exposure Techniques

- Use progressive exposure techniques to help the patient gradually confront the specific phobia. Develop a hierarchy of phobia-related situations, from the least anxiety-provoking to the most anxiety-provoking, and guide the patient in gradually exposing themselves to these situations.

Example: If the patient has a fear of spiders, start with exposure to images of spiders, then move on to videos, and eventually encourage real-life encounters with spiders under controlled supervision.

Step 5: Relaxation Techniques

- Teach the patient relaxation techniques such as deep breathing, progressive muscle relaxation, or meditation to help reduce the anxiety associated with the specific phobia.

Example: Guide the patient to practice deep breathing exercises when exposed to phobia-related situations, promoting relaxation and reducing anxiety reactions.

Step 6: Positive Reinforcement and Maintenance

- Encourage the patient to regularly practice the learned techniques and recognize the progress made. Use positive reinforcement to reward efforts and maintain the gains achieved.

Example: Congratulate the patient for each successful step of exposure and encourage them to continue exposing themselves to phobia-related situations to maintain progress.

By following these steps, you will be able to effectively apply CBT in the treatment of specific phobias. Identifying irrational thoughts, using progressive exposure techniques, and learning relaxation strategies are key elements in helping patients overcome their specific phobias and regain an improved quality of life.

These specific applications of cognitive-behavioral therapy illustrate its versatility and adaptability in treating a variety of psychological issues. CBT provides concrete techniques and strategies to help individuals overcome their difficulties and improve their mental and emotional well-being

Conclusion

In conclusion, cognitive-behavioral therapy is a powerful and effective approach for the treatment of psychological problems. It is based on the idea that our thoughts, emotions, and behaviors are interconnected, and by modifying these aspects, we can improve our mental and emotional well-being.

This book has explored the fundamental principles of cognitive-behavioral therapy, providing a comprehensive and pragmatic understanding of this approach. We have examined the foundations of cognitive-behavioral therapy, including the cognitive model, the behavioral model, and the integrated approach.

We have also explored specific cognitive and behavioral techniques used in CBT, such as identifying automatic thoughts, cognitive restructuring, exposure and response prevention, behavioral activation, relaxation techniques, social skills training, and many more.

Furthermore, we have explored specific applications of CBT, including the treatment of anxiety, depression, eating disorders, obsessive-compulsive disorders, personality disorders, sleep disorders, stress management, addictions, time management issues, and specific phobias.

Finally, we have delved into treatment planning and setting therapeutic goals, as well as relapse management and prevention. These elements are crucial in guiding the therapeutic process, measuring progress, and maintaining the achieved results.

Cognitive-behavioral therapy offers practical and concrete tools to help individuals understand and modify their thought patterns, emotions, and behaviors, leading to an overall improvement in mental and emotional well-being. Whether you are a beginner in the field of CBT or seeking to deepen your knowledge, this book has provided you with a solid foundation to further explore and apply this approach in your daily life.

Whether it's overcoming anxiety, depression, eating disorders, or other challenges, cognitive-behavioral therapy can provide you with the tools and resources needed to thrive.

Made in United States
North Haven, CT
12 June 2024

53513921R10055